Authentic

DEVOTION

Jacquelyn Jessen
1305 Donels Dr
Vinton, IA 52349

Introduction to the Devout Life
by FRANCIS DE SALES

Authentic
DEVOTION

A Modern Interpretation by
Bernard Bangley

SHAW BOOKS
an imprint of WATERBROOK PRESS

Authentic Devotion
A SHAW BOOK
PUBLISHED BY WATERBROOK PRESS
2375 Telstar Drive, Suite 160
Colorado Springs, Colorado 80920
A division of Random House, Inc.

All Scripture quotations, unless otherwise indicated, are taken from the *Holy Bible, New International Version*®. NIV®. Copyright © 1973, 1978, 1984 by International Bible Society. Used by permission of Zondervan Publishing House. All rights reserved. Scripture quotations marked *(Anchor Bible)* are taken from *The Anchor Bible, Old Testament Apocrypha,* copyright © 1979 by Doubleday & Company, Inc. All rights reserved. Scripture quotations marked (CEV) are taken from the *Contemporary English Version.* Copyright © 1991, 1992, 1995 by American Bible Society. Used by permission. Scripture quotations marked (KJV) are taken from the *King James Version.* Scripture quotations marked (NRSV) are from the *New Revised Standard Version of the Bible,* copyright © 1989 by the Division of Christian Education of the National Council of the Churches of Christ in the USA. Used by permission. All rights reserved. Scripture quotations marked (TEV) are from the *Today's English Version*—Second Edition. Copyright © 1992 by American Bible Society. Used by permission.

ISBN 0-87788-000-X

SHAW BOOKS and its aspen leaf logo are trademarks of WaterBrook Press, a division of Random House, Inc.

Library of Congress Cataloging-in-Publication Data
   Bangley, Bernard, 1935–
      Authentic devotion : a modern interpretation of Introduction to the devout life by Francis de Sales /
   Bernard Bangley. —1st ed.
         p. cm.
   "A Shaw book."
      ISBN 0-87788-000-X
      1. Francis, de Sales, Saint, 1567–1622. Introduction a la vie devote. 2. Meditations. 3. Spiritual life—
   Catholic Church. I. Title.
      BX2179.F83 B36 2002
      248.4'82—dc21

                                                                              2002006536

Printed in the United States of America
2002—First Edition

10 9 8 7 6 5 4 3 2 1

For Jonathan, Kate, Logan, and Sarah,
with the prayer that they and their generation will discover
the depth of spirituality described in this book.

✛

Contents

Timeline of the Life of Francis de Sales ix

Introduction by Bernard Bangley 1

Introduction to the Devout Life

Prayer of Dedication 11

Preface 13

Instructions for Beginning to Fully Living the Devout Life 15

The Value of Prayer and Sacraments 31

The Challenge of Christian Living 45

Temptations and Setbacks 91

Renewing the Spiritual Life 105

Timeline of the Life of Francis de Sales

August 21, 1567	Born in Thorens, Savoy
1580–88	Studied in Paris
1591	Earned doctorate in law at University of Padua
1593	Ordained as a priest
1595	Attempted assassination of Francis
1597	Pope Clement VIII dispatched Francis to Geneva, Switzerland, where Francis almost countered the Calvinistic movement
1602	Became bishop of Geneva
1604	Met Jane de Chantal and became her spiritual director
1607	Begins to write *Treatise of the Love of God* (coincided with the founding of the Jamestown settlement)
1609	First edition of *Introduction to the Devout Life* published in France
1619	Revised edition of *Introduction to the Devout Life* published
December 28, 1622	Died in Lyons, France

In 1665, Francis de Sales was canonized as a saint, and in 1877, he was declared Doctor of the Church. For more information about Francis de Sales, visit the Web site of the Francis de Sales Resource Center: www.desalesresource.org.

Introduction

Francis de Sales (1567–1622) was bishop of Geneva, Switzerland, during the lifetime of many first-generation Protestant Calvinists. During this time there was a distrust and bitter rejection of Roman Catholicism. As a bishop, Francis had to set up shop outside the city. He worked among a hostile public who had little interest in his message. At times, emotional crowds endangered his life. Francis was perfectly equipped for his station, however. He possessed the qualities of a diplomat of the highest order. His gentle warmth disarmed any potential critic. His profound spirituality and commitment to Jesus was convincing evidence of authenticity. His gentle, patient, honest spirituality was a valuable asset to all Christians during those turbulent years. Like Francis of Assisi, Francis de Sales was not the kind of personality that would invite any kind of hostile exchange.

His gentleness was evidenced through his pen as well as his presence. With a clear and orderly mind, he expressed himself in terms that were quickly understood. It was natural for him to put his ideas on paper, and those offerings have benefited thousands over the past four hundred years.

The works of Saint Francis de Sales have been collected in a massive twenty-seven volumes. This definitive compilation of his works began in 1892 and continued through 1964 at the religious community he founded (with Jane de Chantal) in Annecy, France, a short distance south of Geneva. A warm humanity radiates from every page of the voluminous writings.

Francis's *Introduction to the Devout Life* began as a series of letters of spiritual guidance to Mme de Charmoisy, wife of the ambassador of the duke of Savoy. Legal complications required Mme de Charmoisy to reside for a while in Annecy, where Francis was attracting many who were seeking spiritual direction. She also sought his guidance. When she returned home a few months later, they continued their spiritual relationship through the mail. His letters overflowed with sane, profound, spiritual insight combined with an extraordinary understanding of human psychology. She was so impressed with his instruction that she showed it to the rector of the College of Chambery. He shared her estimate of the value of the material and urged Francis to have it published. Francis made a few minor revisions, such as addressing the reader as "Philothea" (Lover of God) and incorporating material from some of his letters to others. The work was published in 1609 and was immediately recognized as one of the truly great masterpieces of devotional literature. It was translated into many languages and was printed in several editions during the saint's lifetime.

While Francis makes no claim for any originality of thought, he does admit that he has brought those spiritual insights together in a fresh way. In fact, his careful style and his constant awareness of the limitations of his readers, combined with a unique talent for apt illustration, make this work far and away the best of its kind. Other writers have said some of the same things, to be sure, but none of them have said them in *this* way and with such symmetry and naturalness.

Francis's references to nature, sometimes more fanciful than factual, are part of what make the *Introduction* sparkle with life. In a letter that is now printed under the title *On the Preacher and Preaching*, Francis comments upon the value of illustration, or "comparisons." He writes, "They have great power to aid understanding and to motivate the will." He cites Christ's ability to teach great truth with something as simple as seeds. Much of Francis's nature lore is taken from classical authors such as Aristotle, Pliny, and Dioscorides. We can be sure that honeybees do not carry little stones for ballast in a storm. Neither is a mountain rabbit white in winter because all it sees or eats is snow. The points Francis makes with such challengeable illustrations from nature are nonetheless precisely applicable to the facts of the spiritual life. Scientific accuracy becomes unimportant. (In 1987 I was invited to speak to a national gathering of Catholics who are devoted to keeping Francis's teachings in the forefront of modern spirituality. After my talk, a sister presented me with a very special gift. It was a fuzzy black-and-yellow bee. Nothing could have been more appropriate.) Francis warns, however, against the use of substandard material. "The preacher must be careful not to tell about false miracles and nonsensical tales which are common enough in popular books. Such things will make us deserve scorn and criticism."

One of the features of the *Introduction* is its insistence upon using the services of a spiritual director. Francis's early biographer, Jean Pierre Camus, discusses this topic with him personally, and we are privileged to have Francis's own amplification of the concept in the *Introduction* itself. Camus writes, "I once asked Francis who his spiritual director was. He pulled *Spiritual Combat* from his pocket, explaining, 'This little book has been the Director of my inner life since I was young.' I reminded him that in his *Introduction* he wrote of having a living Director. 'You are correct,' he said, 'but remember that I also said he would be difficult to find. We can look for guidance among the books of authors who are no longer living. Devotional books are our best Directors. But when we can't understand what we read we should consult with those who are familiar with the language of the mystics. But there is no advantage to always consulting with the same individual. As the Scripture says, "In a multitude of counsellors there is safety" (Proverbs 11:14, KJV).'" We know that in Francis's younger years, a Jesuit father named Possevin was his spiritual director. Francis later became the quintessential spiritual director for many others. He has been called "the Saint Maker." After personally examining him before the Sacred College for a special appointment, Pope Clement VIII accurately predicted that many would be helped by the waters that would flow from his spiritual fountain.

An often-related anecdote comes from the time Camus was working closely with Francis. Camus privately wondered if the saint actually practiced what he preached. Using a peephole to spy on him when he was alone, Camus was astonished to discover that the man's private behavior was as beautiful as his life in public. He observed Francis waking quietly in order to let his valet sleep a little longer. Then there were times of private prayer, writing, breakfast, and more prayer. The elegance and Christian gentleness that astonished others continued at all times of day. He was as courteous to a cleaning lady as he was to a prince. In no way could he have thought that the devout life he described in this book was unlivable. He lived it himself. He lived it with an astonishing ease that authenticated every detail.

OUTLINE OF *LA VIE DEVOTE*

A classic masterpiece of spiritual writing, *Introduction to the Devout Life (La Vie Devote)*, is acknowledged to be among the top handful of guides to the Christian life. It takes the reader by the hand. A person at almost any stage of spiritual development is gently guided down the clearest path imaginable into a deeper and more authentic religious life.

Introduction to the Devout Life connects devotion with ordinary daily living. It is not written for cloistered monks. It is directed to people whose spiritual life must survive and prosper in a secular environment. No other title in its genre comes close to its practical, honest, simple, gentle guidance into an awareness of God's presence and activity in the ordinary world.

Francis de Sales divides his book into five sections. The first section presents clear and precise guidance from early in the devout life to fully living a devout life. His instructions on how to meditate are remarkably understandable and can be practiced by anyone without previous experience or professional guidance.

This first section offers a greater understanding of how one can be both active and meditative. In recent years, many Westerners have turned to the spirituality of the East, thinking that Christianity had nothing to offer for those who wanted to practice peaceful contemplation. Turning to other religions, however, trades rich prayer for self-focused meditation that is void of Christ. Francis de Sales is a beautiful example of a devout Christian who practiced meditation as part of his commitment to the Lord. Even the most inexperienced and dense among us have little difficulty following the technique he describes. Most important, it works. It is the foundation of a completely satisfying and useful prayer life.

The second section of Francis's book affirms the value of prayer and sacrament while elaborating on the method described in the first section. Francis encourages us to spend more time in honest prayer and teaches us to make the most of both silent and spoken prayer. His instruction on meditation is superb, and it will take you as deep as you care to go, without letting you get lost in unhealthy pretenses.

The third part of *La Vie Devote* contains a series of lessons on virtuous behavior—challenges to Christian living. Some of the topics may seem rather quaint to modern readers. Francis gives advice on a Christian's relationship to card playing, dancing, clothes, language, and gambling. While some readers may feel that the advice belongs in a museum, it must still be conceded that the writer is telling the truth, and that his assessment of the gains and losses in each case is accurate. For instance, there is no way we can take issue with this: "The only pleasure in gambling is winning, and that pleasure results from another's loss and pain. This is certainly evil." Or this: "Balls and dances are recreations that are morally neutral, but the manner in which they are conducted can push them toward hazardous evil." Every page of this section is worthy of careful consideration.

The fourth part of the book describes and addresses the temptations and setbacks that naturally affect anyone setting out on the devout life. There is a unique honesty here. Francis acknowledges that all of us are human and that he is no exception to that fact. He looks at what we sweep under the rug, declares those things are not surprising, and tells us how to overcome them—or how to live with them if we can't eliminate them from our experience. No one will ever put this book down feeling discouraged or outclassed.

The final section deals with the important business of continually renewing the spiritual life. Francis reviews important points made earlier, firmly nailing them down in our consciousness. A reader finishing the last page has a feeling of having been in the man's gentle presence and has a strong desire to read the book again.

The Approach of this Interpretation

Accurate English translations of the complete *Introduction to the Devout Life* are available, but these can be difficult reading for many today. The antique style is a barrier for uninitiated modern readers. John Ryan rendered a highly respected English translation in 1950. His thorough work was published in several versions over a span of years and remains available today. If my simplified version stimulates your interest, you cannot do better than to seek a copy of Ryan's work.

Others have made efforts to modernize Francis de Sales by adapting his ideas in a style that barely resembles the original material. My approach has been to keep the content of the book entirely that of Francis de Sales. I have introduced no idea, insight, or metaphor of my own. This present volume is what I prefer to call an "honest paraphrase." Reading these easy pages will give you an actual experience of the original.

In his original work, Francis does not cite references, assuming that scholars don't need them and general readers would ignore them. Footnotes do tend to clutter and distract. Following his example, I have been very conservative when it comes to adding references to a text that had none. When a large portion of a verse of Scripture is quoted, I place the source in parentheses. Francis assures us that his use of Scripture is not to explain the sacred text but to let it elucidate the point he is trying to make. Unless another version is noted, all Scripture quotations are from the *New International Version.*

Introduction to the Devout Life does contain some seventeenth-century concepts that modern readers may find confusing. For instance, in today's practical environment, even children know the heart is a blood pump. We do not immediately understand the ancient concept of the heart as the center of love, emotion, and devotion. Francis employs the metaphor of the heart to illustrate the love of God as well as an individual's love for God and neighbor. Scripture provides the basis for this idea. Francis also shows us how the heart can be used to describe and understand God himself.

Also, many people today are not familiar with the original meaning of a *nosegay*. One of the dominant characteristics of life in earlier times was the presence of foul odors. We were slow to learn lessons of sanitation and personal hygiene. Chickens, horses, and other livestock littered the world with their droppings. A stench was in the air. To combat this, people sometimes gathered a fistful of sweetly fragrant flowers. They carried this nostril cheering (hence, "nosegay") bouquet around with them, sniffing its perfume from time to time. Francis makes a clever application of this to the spiritual life. Like Christ who told his parable of the soils and explained what he meant later, Francis presents the concept of a spiritual nosegay matter-of-factly in the first section of the book and comments upon it in greater detail in a subsequent section.

Francis presents Catholic, Protestant, and spiritually seeking readers with universal truths. At the same time, nothing is to be gained by attempting to hide the fact that Saint Francis de Sales was Roman Catholic. There remain in this version many references that tie his point of reference to Catholicism. Even so, the Catholic Church today has changed. Confession, for instance, has become the sacrament of reconciliation. In a very few instances, I slightly neutralize the terminology in order to communicate more freely with a diverse readership.

While most of the subjects Francis de Sales discusses are included in this volume, I have skipped a few. I have omitted topics that do not apply with uniformity to everyone who would live a devout life in a secular environment.

Preparing this modernization has blessed me as I worked. The saint from a time long gone by has repeatedly reached out and touched my heart. His ideas are so absolutely correct and his manner of communicating them so utterly disarming, I was personally shaken time after time. There can be no doubt that my personal life of devotion has been pushed a notch higher by the wise counsel of a man I wish I had known. May he do as much for you as you read.

Introduction to the Devout Life

Prayer of Dedication

Dear Jesus, my Lord, Savior and God, look down on me as I dedicate this book as a tribute to you. Bless it. Make it helpful to others. Let it inspire them as they read. Protect me from failing to be and do the things I recommend. May we sing together, "Vive, Jésus! Live, Jesus!"

— *Saint Francis de Sales, 1609*

Preface

With flowers from the same garden, a flower arranger can create many different designs. This book contains nothing that has not already been said by others. I have picked the same flowers. The difference is in the way I present them.

Most devotional guides are prepared for individuals who are living a sheltered life apart from the everyday world. I want to teach the practice of devotion to ordinary people who work in a secular environment and live in town with their families.

Some may think this is not possible. It is certainly not easy, but it can be done. This book is presented as a guide to anyone, in any situation, who wants to live a life of devotion to God.

I began this project by writing letters to a particular woman who seriously desired to live a devout life. She showed them to someone who thought they would be helpful to many others. He pleaded with me to publish this private instruction in book form.

It took time I really didn't have to organize and revise this material. I was much too busy to worry about writing anything fancy. Instead, I tried to present worthwhile thought in simple language.

As I wrote, I did not think of myself as addressing a large crowd but as quietly talking with one person. Because I know this will reach many souls, I invented a nickname representing an individual who seeks the love of God through a life of devotion. *Philothea* means "Lover of God."

The book is in five parts:

1. Instructions for beginning to fully living the devout life
2. The value of prayer and sacraments
3. The challenge of Christian living

4. Temptations and setbacks

5. Renewing the spiritual life

Many will object that I am mistaken to present these ideas to the general public. They will also accuse me of being too busy with my work as a bishop to concentrate on these things. My reply is that it is a bishop's responsibility to offer such guidance to all the souls in his care. There could be no better use of any spare time I manage to find.

I admit I am teaching before I am fully competent. It is my hope that the devotion I wish to instill in others may also grow in me.

Francis de Sales
Annecy, France, 1609

Instructions for Beginning
to Fully Living the Devout Life

True devotion must be sought among many counterfeits. People naturally think their way is best. The person who fasts thinks this makes him very devout, even though he may harbor hatred in his heart. Another is a total abstainer from drink who tricks and cheats his neighbor, drinking, as it were, his neighbor's blood. Another is sure he is devout because he says many prayers, and yet his language is arrogant and abrasive at home and at work. Another forgives his enemies but doesn't pay his bills. All these could be thought of as devout, but they are not. They only hint at devotion.

Genuine devotion is simply honest love of God. When this love becomes so much a part of us that we automatically do deliberate good, then it can be labeled *devotion*.

Ostriches are not flying birds. Chickens fly short distances with much effort. Eagles, doves, and swallows fly high and far. Sinners are like the ostrich and are earthbound. Good people who have not quite reached devotion are like the chicken. They fly in God's direction, but inefficiently and awkwardly. The devout regularly soar to God. Devotion, then, is a natural nimbleness of spirit.

A person who is recovering from sickness walks only as much as is necessary. The pace is slow and hesitant. Anyone freshly starting on the path of devotion will also be limping. Eventually, like someone who is in good health, you will be walking, running, leaping toward God. "I run in the path of your commands, for you have set my heart free" (Psalm 119:32).

The Israelites were discouraged from entering the Promised Land by reports of the hazards that waited there for them. They were told that the air was bad and that the natives were monsters. In the same way, the world makes noises about holy devotion. It says the devout are long-faced and gloomy. It can only see the outward evidence of prayer, fasting, acts of charity, suppressed anger and passions, self-denial, and other things. These may appear to be painful. The secular world can never see the warmth of inward devotion that transforms such difficult things into joy, just as the bees turn the bitter nectar of thyme into honey. Devotion is a kind of spiritual sugar that removes bitterness from life's experiences.

During the creation of our world, God commanded, "Let the land produce vegetation: seed-bearing plants and trees on the land that bear fruit with seed in it, according to their various kinds" (Genesis 1:11). Now God commands Christians, who are the fruit-bearing branches of his church, to exercise devotion in a manner appropriate to occupation and position. It is not the same for everyone. Devotion is expressed in one way by a laborer and another way by a prince, a young girl, a married woman, or a widow. The manner in which you engage in devotional activities will also depend upon your physical condition, your activities, and your responsibilities. It would make no sense for a skilled craftsman to be in church all day, or for a monk to attend numerous committee meetings. That would result in a comically distorted kind of devotion.

Aristotle noticed that a bee can extract honey from a flower without harming the flower. It leaves them as fresh as it found them. Authentic devotion is even better. Not only does it never interfere with earning a living, it also makes your work more effective. In the same way a stone's particular color and pattern shines when moistened with honey, your occupation will be beautified and enhanced by your devotional life. Love at home will deepen. Being a parent will become more manageable. Any service you render will be more honest and faithful. Every job you do will be more enjoyable.

It is a huge mistake to think that soldiers, merchants, politicians, mechanics, and the like are not able to have a profound devotional life.

Such people would have difficulty praying, worshiping, and studying on the schedule of someone in a cloister, but there are other valid ways to express devotion to God. Wherever you are, whatever you do for a living, you can and should desire to live a devout life.

If you are serious about this, it is very important for you to find a good spiritual director, a faithful friend who can answer your questions and guide you along the proper path. Make your choice carefully. Not one in ten thousand is worthy. Ask God to lead you to such a person. When you find your own, thank God and be on your way together. "Faithful friends are a sturdy shelter: whoever finds one has found a treasure. Faithful friends are beyond price; no amount can balance their worth. Faithful friends are life-saving medicine; and those who fear the Lord will find them" (Sirach 6:14-16, NRSV).

GETTING STARTED

The first step toward the devout life is the cleansing of your soul. "Put away your former way of life...be renewed" (Ephesians 4:22-23, NRSV). Remove anything that stands in the way of your union with God. This will be a gradual process. It has been compared with sunrise, which brings light in imperceptible steps. Darkness is not driven away immediately. The saying is that a slow cure is best. Sicknesses of the soul are like those of the body. They come galloping in on horseback but depart slowly on foot.

Have courage and be patient. Many see themselves as still imperfect after trying to be devout for a long time. It would be a pity to become discouraged and give up because you see so many imperfections in yourself. The only thing worse would be to think that you are already perfect after the first day of throwing away things from your old life. It's like trying to fly without wings. There is a great risk of relapse if we stop seeing the doctor too soon.

Actually, the work of cleansing your soul will go on for a lifetime.

There is no reason to be upset by our imperfections. Our perfection consists of struggling against our imperfection. How can we resist them unless we see them? How can we overcome them unless we face them?

THE FIRST CLEANSING

The first cleansing is confession of sin. Be honest and recall in detail every sin of your life. Write them down if you want. Then with great sorrow admit that you have fallen from grace, given up heaven, chosen hell, and rejected God's love. What I am asking for, Philothea, is a general confession of a lifetime of sin. This is the way to see who you are. It will bring healthy regret for past errors and fill us with gratitude for God's mercy. We will see how patiently he has been waiting for us, and that will calm us and make us want to do better.

THE SECOND CLEANSING

All the Israelites left Egypt, but in the desert many of them had second thoughts and wanted to return. In the same way, some resolve to avoid sin, but they look back at Sodom even while fleeing it. Like a sick man who has been told by his doctor to eliminate melons from his diet, they give up their sins but go right on talking about them, desiring them, and envying those whose diets are not restricted. Philothea, if you want to live a devout life, you are required both to stop sinning and to lose your appetite for it.

To arrive at this, meditate in the following manner. With God's help, these steps will pluck both the sin and the desire for it out of your heart. Follow the order in which I have given them, one a day. It is best to do this in the morning and then reflect upon them during the remainder of the day. If you are not familiar with meditating, there is some help for you in the second part of this book.

1. MEDITATION ON OUR CREATION

Preparation

Place yourself in God's presence.

Ask God to inspire you.

Thoughts

Think of the time before you were born. Where was your soul then? The world existed, but it saw nothing of you.

Out of his goodness, God pulled you out of that void and made you who you are.

Think of the possibilities God has placed in you.

Responses and Resolutions

Be humble before God. "O my soul, you would still be a part of that nothingness if God had not pulled you out of it. You would be neither conscious nor active."

Thank God. "My good Creator, I owe you a tremendous debt. You made me what I am. How can I ever express my thanks?"

Reprimand yourself. "I have run far away from my Creator and sinned. I have not respected his goodness. Beginning now, I will admit that I am nothing. How can dust and ashes take pride in itself? I want to change my life. I will follow my Creator."

Conclusion

Thank God. Offer yourself to him. Ask him to help you keep your resolutions.

When you have finished your prayer, go back through it and pick a few flowers.

Make a devotional nosegay, a spiritual bouquet to enjoy all day long.

2. Meditation on the Purpose of Life

Preparation

Place yourself in God's presence.

Ask God to inspire you.

Thoughts

God did not put you in the world because he needed you. He made you for the purpose of working his goodness in you by giving you his grace. He has given you a mind to know him, a memory to recall his favors, a will to love him, eyes to see what he does, a tongue to sing his praise. This is the reason you are here. Anything that hinders it must be avoided.

Think of the unhappy people who miss this point and live as though they were here only to construct houses, plant trees, accumulate money, and waste themselves on the trifling.

Responses and Resolutions

Scold your soul with humility. Remind it that until now it has been so miserable that it hasn't thought much about these things. Ask yourself, "What did I think about when I did not think about God? What did I remember when I forgot God? What did I love when I did not love God?"

Hate your previous behavior. "I am through thinking shallow thoughts and making futile plans. I renounce bad friendships, ugly deeds, and self-indulgence."

Turn to God. "My Savior, from now on you will regularly be in my thoughts. I will stop thinking about evil things. I will remember your mercy toward me every day. The vanities I used to chase after now disgust me."

Conclusion

Thank God for your purpose in life. Ask him to help you to measure up to it.

Pick some spiritual flowers.

3. MEDITATION ON GOD'S BLESSINGS

Preparation

Place yourself in God's presence.

Ask God to inspire you.

Thoughts

God has blessed you with a body and everything necessary to sustain life. Think of those less fortunate than yourself.

Think about the clarity and capacity of your mind. God has blessed you. Remember that some are not so fortunate.

Think about your spiritual blessings, Philothea. You grew up in the church. You have heard about God from childhood. Notice the small things and see how gentle and kind God has been in your life.

Responses and Resolutions

Let God's goodness astonish you. "How good God has been to me! How merciful! How generous!"

Let your gratefulness astonish you. "Why did you care about me, Lord? I am not worthy. I have thrown your blessings away like so much trash. I have not been thankful for it all."

Declare a resolution. "I resolve to stop being unfaithful, ungrateful, and disloyal to God."

Go to church. "I will pray and observe the sacraments. I will hear your holy word and make it a part of my life."

Conclusion

Thank God for what you see now. Offer your heart to him. Ask him to help you keep your promises.

Pick a little spiritual bouquet.

4. MEDITATION ON SIN

Preparation

Place yourself in God's presence.

Ask him to inspire you.

Thoughts

Remember when you first began to sin and how your sins increased over the years. Think about your sins toward God, yourself, your neighbors. Think about the things you have done, spoken, desired, fantasized.

Think about how lightly you have handled holy things and how you have run to escape God even as he was looking for you.

Responses and Resolutions

Let this trouble you. "Dear God, how can I let you see me? Not one day of my life is spotless! Is this how I pay you back?"

Ask God to forgive you. "Like the prodigal son, like Mary Magdalene, I throw myself down before you and ask for mercy on a sinner, my Lord."

Promise to live a better life. "With your help, Lord, I will not sin again. I hate my sin. I will admit each sin and drive it out of my life. I will start by weeding out the most troublesome. I will make amends where I can."

Conclusion

Thank God for patiently waiting for this moment. Offer your heart to him. Ask him to let it be as you have vowed. Seek his strength.

5. Meditation on Death

Preparation

Place yourself in God's presence.

Beg for his grace.

Imagine yourself bedridden with a terminal illness.

Thoughts

Think of the unpredictability of the time of your death. You don't know whether it will be summer or winter, day or night. Will it come suddenly or with time to prepare? Will it result from sickness or accident? You know nothing about what will kill you or when it will happen. All you know is that you will die.

Think how that will remove you from the world. All the little recreations of life will evaporate. Only God will be important. Small sins will loom like mountains, and your devotion will seem very small.

Think about your soul saying good-bye to your money, clubs, games, friends, parents, children, husband, wife, everyone. See it say good-bye to your body lying there ugly with the pallor of death upon it.

Think of the speed with which others will take that lifeless body out to be buried. And when that job is done, consider how little the world will ever think of you again. It will remember you no more than you have thought of others who have died.

Think about where your soul will go after leaving your body. Which path will it take? It will travel the same road it started to travel in this world.

Responses and Resolutions

Run to God and let him hug you. "Lord, look out for me when I die. Make it a good experience."

Have no attachment to this world. "World, you are nothing ultimate for me. I have no permanent relationship with you."

Conclusion

Thank God. Offer your desires to him. Ask him to make your death happy in Christ.

Gather a bouquet of myrrh.

6. Meditation on Judgment

Preparation

Place yourself in God's presence.

Ask God to inspire you.

Thoughts

When earthly time has run out, this planet will be reduced to ashes by a raging fire. Nothing will escape.

Think about the frightening words Scripture speaks to the evil, "Depart from me, you who are cursed, into the eternal fire prepared for the devil and his angels" (Matthew 25:41).

Think about the opposite command that is spoken to the good, "Come, you who are blessed by my Father; take your inheritance, the kingdom prepared for you since the creation of the world" (Matthew 25:34).

Responses and Resolutions

Let these thoughts trouble you deeply. "O God, who will make me secure on the Day of Judgment?"

Judge yourself—now. "I will look for those things that stain my conscience and condemn them for you in advance, O Lord. I will confess my sins."

Conclusion

Thank God. Offer him a penitent heart.

Gather a bouquet.

7. MEDITATION ON HELL

Preparation
Place yourself in God's presence.
Humbly seek God's help.
Imagine a dreary place crowded with trapped people.

Thoughts
There is a punishment that suits the crime.
Beyond all imaginable grief there is separation from God.
If an insect or a fever can make the night seem long, this eternal darkness is raw terror.

Responses and Resolutions
Let the words of Isaiah make you tremble. "Who of us can dwell with the consuming fire? Who of us can dwell with everlasting burning?" (Isaiah 33:14). It is unbearable to consider being permanently separated from God.

Admit that you deserve hell. "But from now on, Lord, I will be on another road. I have no desire for a trip to destruction."

Think of some specific ways you can improve your life. What can you do to protect yourself from temptation?

Conclusion
Thank God. Pray.

8. MEDITATION ON HEAVEN

Preparation
Place yourself in God's presence.
Appeal to his greater power.

Thoughts

Imagine a clear, gorgeous night with a star-filled sky. Without losing that image, consider the beauty of a really nice day. Put it all together and you will still not have anything that compares with heaven.

Think about all the good souls that inhabit heaven. Picture angels by the million. Such radiance! Such music! Such joy!

They are blessed forever.

Responses and Resolutions

Let it impress you. "You are beautiful, dear Jerusalem. There is nothing but happiness here."

Rebuke yourself for every step you have ever taken on a road in some other direction than here.

Let it attract you.

Conclusion

Thank God. Pray.

9. THE DECISION TO LIVE DEVOUTLY

Preparation

Place yourself in God's presence.

Humbly ask him to inspire this moment.

Thoughts

Think what it would be like to be alone in a big meadow. Your guardian angel is with you and shows you all heaven open before you as you conceived it in your last meditation. There below you is hell with all its torments. You are right in the middle. Both heaven and hell beckon.

The choice is yours.

Your decision has eternal consequences.

God will grant you hell with his justice or heaven with his mercy.

Something more important is at work here. God is eager for you to choose heaven. In a way you can barely imagine, God desires this for you. He will provide you with incredible grace and assistance.

Jesus Christ mercifully invites you. "Come join me, here. I have lovingly prepared a place for you."

His mother sighs as your own mother would. "Listen to my Son."

Countless holy souls beg you to join them in praising and loving God. They explain that it is not as difficult to become one of them as you might think. They offer words of encouragement. "You can do it."

Decision

I despise everything related to evil. I turn toward heaven.

I accept God's mercy.

I accept Christ's invitation.

My motive is love.

I accept heaven's help.

Continue to work with me until I become a one of those who devoutly love you. I want to join that heavenly chorus in shouting, "*Vive, Jésus!* Live Jesus!"

HONEST WITH GOD

There remain some important meditations, Philothea. There is nothing to be hesitant about. The poison of a scorpion can be turned into its own antidote. A sin is bad when it is committed, but confession and repentance transform it. Repentance and confession are lovely. They can override ugliness. Simon the leper characterized Mary Magdalene as a sinner. Our Lord disagreed. He was pleased with her humble act of anointing him with expensive perfume. If we are unhappy about what we have done because we know God is displeased, the behavior takes on a new character.

It is important to tell the doctor exactly what our symptoms are. Be completely honest with God. Tell it all, candidly and sincerely. This will greatly relieve your conscience. Then listen obediently for any guidance. Pray, "Speak, LORD, for your servant is listening" (1 Samuel 3:9). God will speak to you through your director. "He who listens to you listens to me" (Luke 10:16).

Now prepare yourself to enter into a serious agreement with God. Read the next section very carefully. Spend some time meditating upon it before you sign it. This is a way to bring closure.

A Contract Between a Soul and God

In God's presence, and with the court of heaven as witness, I admit that I have failed in many ways to live up to the potential that is in me. I confess the sin I abhor and humbly ask for grace and pardon. This is the only hope I have. I renew my vow of faith and renounce all evil. I resolve to serve and love God forever. To him I dedicate my mind, my heart, my body. If I should succumb to temptation and fail to keep this contract, I will, with the help of the Holy Spirit, stop as soon as I see what is happening and return to God's mercy without delay.

This is my desire and my resolution. I sign it now without reservation or exception.

_____

(signed)

Almighty God, help me to keep this sacrifice of my heart. As you have inspired me to do this, give me the strength to keep it. Live, Jesus!

FINISHING THE FIRST CLEANSING

Now be still and listen. Listen inwardly for the Savior's assurance of pardon. Experience the joyous celebration of the angels in heaven. "I tell you, there is rejoicing in the presence of the angels of God over one sinner who repents" (Luke 15:10). You will receive the kiss of peace and fellowship.

Your soul is restored. God is merciful. You have made a treaty with God. He will set himself "like a seal over your heart" (Song of Songs 8:6).

You will still have struggles. I am going to give you some guidance that will keep you from ever stumbling again, if you take it seriously. Sin will not have a chance with you. Spiritual purity is a possibility for you.

But first let me describe the total cleanliness we desire. The low angle of the sun early in the morning reveals the wrinkles on our faces. As daylight reveals our imperfections, the internal light of the Holy Spirit lights our conscience. We see our sins more distinctly. At the same time, we are inspired to improve. You will discover that you are not entirely free of attraction to the less than desirable. There remains a proclivity to sin. We are never entirely free from these tendencies, but we can stop having affection for them. It is not the same to lie occasionally in some unimportant banter as it is to enjoy lying habitually about serious matters.

"Little" sins are not in harmony with devotion. They drain the spirit's power. They interfere with what God is trying to do in you. They open doors to greater sins. While they are not spiritually lethal, they can still bring sickness. Spiders are not deadly to bees, but they entangle their honeycombs with webs and make their work difficult. Excusable sins will not destroy your soul, but if they wrap a tangle of bad habits around you, devotion will suffer. Philothea, it is not earthshaking to tell a small lie or to say or do something slightly risqué or to dress, joke, play, or dance with a little freedom—as long as you don't allow these spiritual spiders to spin their webs and ruin the hive of your conscience. While it is not wrong to have a little harmless fun, it can become dangerous. The evil is not in the pastimes; it is in our affection for them. Children enjoy chasing butterflies. That is what children are supposed to do. It is tragic when we grow up and continue to chase the valueless trifles mentioned above. Don't sow weeds in the soil of your heart. Your garden space is limited.

Evil habits can corrupt the best person, but God's grace (if we cooperate) can improve the worst. Here, then, are the instructions that will show you how to get rid of your desire for them.

The Value of Prayer
and Sacraments

Prayer is the most effective means at our disposal for the cleansing of our mind and emotions. This is because it places the first in God's bright light and the other in God's warm love. Prayer is like a stream of water that nourishes the plants that are our best intentions, and prayer is also able to extinguish the fires of passion that burn within us.

Best of all is silent, inward prayer, especially if it reflects upon our Lord's loving sacrifice. If you think of him frequently, he will occupy your soul. You will catch on to his manner of living and thinking. You will begin to live and think like him. He is "the light of the world" (John 8:12). He is our instructor and our example. It is exactly parallel to the way children learn to talk by listening to their mothers and then making sounds with their own voices. If we remain close to our Savior by meditating upon the things he said and did, we will begin to speak and behave more in his manner.

Philothea, there is no other way in. Prayer is essential. A mirror would not reflect our image if its glass were not backed by something shiny. In the same way, we will never succeed in contemplating God unless our effort is backed up by thoughts of our Lord's divine humanity. The best subjects for our meditation are his life and death. Jesus said, "I am the bread that came down from heaven" (John 6:41). In the same way that bread accompanies a meal with a variety of foods, meditation on our Savior's life and death is a staple for every moment of prayer. Many good guides have been published to assist you in this.

Find an hour each day, in the morning if possible, and pray. Early in the morning your mind will be fresher and less preoccupied with other business. Unless you are specifically directed to do so, do not continue this prayer beyond an hour. It can be helpful to do this in the sanctuary of a church. It will be quiet, and you will be less likely to be interrupted.

Start every prayer with an awareness of the presence of God. Be strict about this, and you will soon see its value. Don't rush through your prayers. The Lord's Prayer said once with comprehension is better than many prayers said in haste.

There are other aids to prayer (such as the rosary) that can be helpful if you know how to use them correctly. But if you can do it, inward, silent prayer is best. If you are reciting a standard prayer and find your heart being drawn deeper, by all means leave the one and go after the other. Don't worry about leaving your spoken prayer unfinished. Your silent prayer pleases God the most, and it will be better for your soul.

Be diligent about this. Don't let a morning pass without some time in silent prayer. If the demands of business or some other responsibility prevents it, then be sure to repair the damage that evening. At the very least, read something from a devotional book and pray short prayers. Make a vow to resume your regular practice of morning prayer again tomorrow.

A SIMPLE WAY TO MEDITATE

Perhaps you are not able to pray silently. Many people today are poor at this. I am showing you an easy way to get started. Do it this way until you have read more widely and gained more experience. Let's look more closely at these preliminary steps.

First, place yourself in God's presence. Consider how God is present in all things and in all places. Wherever the birds fly, they are constantly in the air. Wherever we go, God is always there. Instead of merely assenting to this, it is necessary to make the realization of its truth live for us. Someone who is blind will not see a member of royalty enter a room. There will be no proper demonstration of respect until someone announces that royalty is present. Even then, blindness allows such a person to forget. Since we can't see God physically present, we need to activate our consciousness. We might agree to a theological statement about the presence of God, but we don't really perceive it as a fact. Before praying, it is necessary to remind ourselves of God's actual presence. A good way to do this is with Bible verses: "If I go up to the heavens, you are there; if I make my bed in the depths, you are there" (Psalm 139:8); "Surely the LORD is in this place, and I was not aware of it.... How awesome is this place! This is none other than the house of God; this is the gate of heaven" (Genesis 28:16-17). When you pray, begin by sincerely addressing yourself: "God is here with me. God is really near to me."

Second, ask God to inspire you. Remember that God is not only where you are, he is also actually in your heart, in the core of your spirit. The divine presence in you is what gives you life and inspiration. "For in him we live and move and have our being" (Acts 17:28). Let this idea stimulate you.

Then think about our Savior watching his children at prayer. "Look! There he stands behind our wall, gazing through the windows, peering through the lattice" (Song of Songs 2:9).

You can use your imagination. Sometimes a circumstance will cause us to say we can imagine an acquaintance participating in a certain activity. "It's like I can *see* him enjoying this."

These are ways you can place yourself in the presence of God as you begin to pray. Try only one of them at a time, and don't dwell on it.

Asking God to inspire you is a prayer of invocation. You already know God is present. With great reverence, your soul bows before his majesty and asks for help. "Do not cast me from your presence or take your Holy Spirit from me" (Psalm 51:11). "Let your face shine on your servant" (Psalm 31:16). "I am your servant; give me discernment that I may understand your statutes" (Psalm 119:125).

There is an additional possibility for preparation. It has been termed "the interior lesson." Imagine the scene you are meditating upon as though it were actually taking place in front of you. Place yourself, for instance, at the foot of the cross. In the same way a cage restricts a bird, this will prevent your mind from wandering. I recommend these things for beginners, Philothea. The more subtle methods are for later.

After the imagination has helped you to prepare yourself begin to meditate intellectually. Choose a subject and begin to follow the thoughts as I have suggested. If a particular thought catches your interest, stay with it. The bees do not flit from flower to flower. They stay until they have gathered all the honey they can from each. If you find nothing for you after trying a particular thought, move on to the next. But don't rush the process. Take your time.

Meditation will naturally make you feel love of God and neighbor, as well as compassion, joy, sorrow, fear, confidence, and the like. Go ahead and let it happen. But don't stop with such generalized responses. Change them into specific resolutions. For instance, you may be meditating upon our Lord's first word from the cross. This will certainly move you to forgive your personal enemies. But that is a small thing unless you go on to say, "Next time, I won't let ———— bother me so much. I will do everything I can to win that person's love." This will help you correct your faults quickly, Philothea. Without that specific last step, your progress will be much slower.

Conclude your meditation with humble thanks and an offering of yourself to God. Offer prayers then gather a devotional nosegay. Let me explain what I mean by that. When people have been strolling through a beautiful garden, they usually pick four or five flowers to take with them through the day. They smell them from time to time to cleanse their nostrils of foul odors. When our souls have roamed in meditation through a spiritual garden, we can choose two or three ideas that seem most helpful and think about them occasionally all day long.

After your time of meditation, immediately begin to put into practice the resolutions you have made. Don't wait another day to get started. Without this application, meditation may be useless or even detrimental. Meditate on a virtue without practicing it, and you will mislead yourself into believing that you have actually become someone you are not. If I have resolved to win the heart of my enemy by being gentle toward that person, I will try to find a way this very day to be friendly to him. If I am not able to see that person face-to-face, I will at least pray for him.

When your silent prayer is over, remain still and quiet for a few moments. Make your transition to other responsibilities gradually. Linger yet awhile in the garden. Walk carefully along the path through the gate so that you won't spill the precious balm you are carrying. Don't be unnatural around other people, but keep as much prayer in you as you can.

There is an art to making the transition from prayer to earning a living. A lawyer must go from prayer to the courtroom, the merchant to his store, a homemaker to her responsibilities—with a gentle motion that will not cause distress. Both prayer and your other duties are gifts from God.

Suppose you are attracted to God as soon as you have gone through the preparation. Then abandon the method I have outlined. The Holy Spirit has already given you the thing you would be seeking in the thoughts. Eventually, the formal steps will blend into a spontaneous unity.

SPIRITUAL DRYNESS

Perhaps there will be a time when you will not experience the pleasures of meditation. Don't let that bother you. In a time like that, return to familiar spoken prayers. Tell God you are sorry and ask him to help you. Kiss a picture of Christ if one is handy. Quote Jacob who said, "I will not let you go unless you bless me" (Genesis 32:26). Or say as the Canaanite woman did to Jesus, "Even the dogs eat the crumbs that fall from their masters' table" (Matthew 15:27).

It could be helpful to begin reading a devotional book. Stick with it until something is triggered in you. Or try some physical motion. If no one can see you, lie flat on the ground. Fold your hands in front of you. Privately hug a crucifix.

If none of these things helps and the spiritual dryness persists, don't despair. The important thing is to persevere. God grants or withholds his favors as he will. Our responsibility is to continue in a devotional manner before him. Our patience will bring pleasure to God. He will not forget our constancy and persistence. Prayer can be a beautiful and extraordinarily pleasant exchange with God. If it is not always such a lofty experience, be satisfied with the knowledge that it is still a high honor to be in God's presence.

MORNING PRAYER

The important formal prayers we say in the course of a day are strengthened by a variety of other brief prayers. There are several subdivisions. Morning prayer is the first. This is when you are getting ready for the day's activity. Here is how it is done.

Worship God. Thank him for allowing you to see another day.

Accept this new day as an opportunity to deepen your spirituality.

Think about the opportunities for service to God that you will have today. Also anticipate the temptations that may come your way. Determine that you will make the best possible use of this new day. Plan ways to evade, oppose, and defeat everything negative. This has got to be more than simply an act of will or desire. Determine now what specific action you will take. For instance, if I know today will include some business with a disagreeable person, I will plan to be careful with my words and demeanor. Perhaps I can think of someone who can help me keep him calm. If this day will include a visit with someone who is sick, I will set a good time for it and think of how I might be of comfort and assistance. I do this for everything that is foreseeable on my schedule.

When you have done this, practice humility in God's presence. Admit that you will not succeed in your plans if you trust your own ability and strength. You will neither escape evil nor perform anything worthwhile on your own. Offer your heart to God. Ask God to protect it and strengthen it. Pray something similar to this: "Lord, take my heart. You have inspired many good intentions in it. It does not have the ability to do what it desires. It needs your blessing. In your mercy, grant your blessing. I want to serve Christ all the days of my life."

All of this can be done fairly quickly. Concentrate fervently. Get it done before you leave your room. Do this every day, Philothea.

EVENING PRAYER

There are two special opportunities for prayer at the end of the day. One is before supper. Let it be a spiritual appetizer. Find a little free time to be alone. Stretch out in God's presence. Let your soul bow before the crucified Christ. You can do this with a simple inward look, or you may review the ideas of your morning prayer, or you may begin a new topic.

The other special moment is before bedtime. Thank God for his care of you this day. Take a serious look at your behavior during the day. Think about specific people and places. If you think you have done something worthwhile, thank God for making it possible. If you discover some utterance, opinion, or action that is unworthy of Christ, seek God's forgiveness. Plan to correct it as soon as possible.

Then place yourself, your family and friends, and the church in God's care. Now you are ready for a good night's sleep. Evening prayer is as necessary as the prayer that begins your day. Morning prayer opens your soul's windows to Christ's sunshine. Evening prayer closes those windows against the darkness of hell.

TURNING ASIDE

I am giving you my best instruction here, Philothea. This is the most helpful thing I know for anyone attempting to make progress spiritually. Keep reminding yourself that you are living in God's presence. Think of God's activity and your own. God is looking upon you with infinite love.

Birds can return to their nests and deer to their thickets. We can select a place near Christ where we can retreat momentarily during the course of our work. Remember to take a few moments inwardly even as you are busy at your occupation. Think of Christ's crucifixion or some other event in his life. Be near him there.

You can actually engage in this solitary behavior while conducting the business of daily life with others. A crowd of people around you will not be able to intrude upon this private act. King David was busy with many responsibilities, and yet he often says in his psalms: "I am always with you; you hold me by my right hand" (Psalm 73:23); "I have set the LORD always before me. Because he is at my right hand, I will not be shaken" (Psalm 16:8); "My eyes are ever on the LORD" (Psalm 25:15).

The parents of Saint Catherine of Siena did not allow her to pray and meditate. She was inspired to construct a small chapel in her soul. She was able to retreat inwardly even while going about ordinary business. When she was later persecuted, Christ steadied her in her interior chapel. She recommended this technique to others.

We will not often be too busy to turn aside to God for an instant. In fact, we can present our souls to him a thousand times a day. Sprinkle a seasoning of short prayers on your daily living. If you see something beautiful, thank God for it. If you are aware of someone's need, ask God to help.

These two things nourish each other. Our desire to be with God is enhanced by time spent with God. Brief, earnest prayers are extremely beneficial. Revel in God's beauty. Let your spirit fall at the base of the cross. Express your love. Converse with him. Reach out like a child for his hand. Hold him close as though he were an aromatic bouquet. Hoist his flag in your heart.

Saint Augustine urged a devout woman to practice such spontaneous prayer. If we become familiar with close, private exchanges with God, the thoughts of our mind will become more beautiful. This is not at all hard to do. You can do it anytime and anywhere. It is not inconvenient even for the busiest person. This little turning aside spiritually is but a moment of relaxation. Instead of interrupting our work, it will help us to work more productively. It is like taking a little refreshment during a journey. Far from interfering with progress, it energizes us. A little rest, and then we can travel better.

Printed collections of quick, impulsive prayers are helpful to many. Verses from the Psalms, the many names of Jesus, the spiritual devotion expressed in the Song of Songs, and religious music function quite well in this regard. My recommendation, though, is that you create your own on the spur of the moment. Such expressions of love can become habitual, like carving a loved one's name on the bark of many trees. Anyone in love with God continuously thinks about God. Such a person wishes it were possible to imprint God's name on everyone's heart. Everything in God's creation is a reminder of God and inspires praise. Let me give you some examples.

Saint Gregory reported in one of his orations that he walked along a beach one day. He noticed the waves deposited shells and seaweed on the sand as they rolled in. When the waves returned to the sea, they swept many of these leavings back out again. Only the great rocks along the beach remained in place even though they were pounded by the waves. He pondered the spiritual lesson being demonstrated. Frail souls are like the shells and seaweed. The strong currents of success and adversity push them around. Brave souls resist storm, tide, and crashing waves. This observation led him to verses from the Psalms: "Save me, O God, for the waters have come up to my neck. I sink in the miry depths, where there is no foothold. I have come into the deep waters; the floods engulf me" (Psalm 69:1-2); "Do not let the floodwaters engulf me or the depths swallow me up or the pit close its mouth over me" (Psalm 69:15).

Saint Francis of Assisi observed a sheep among goats. He said, "Notice how quiet that gentle sheep is. Our Lord behaved the same way among his opponents." On another occasion he looked at a stream of water and prayed, "God's grace flows just as gently and sweetly as this brook."

Someone else stood by a rapidly flowing river and thought, "My soul is as restless as this water. It will not rest until it becomes a part of the divine ocean from which it came." Ordinary things all around you can induce worthy musing and devout yearnings. You can toss up many such prayers all day long. They will help you in your meditation and in your secular employment as well. Make a habit of it.

By all means, go to church. There is always more value for you in public worship than in any private act of devotion. The Lord's Supper is at the very heart of Christianity. Participate in communion as often as possible. Prayers that are combined with bread and cup are extraordinarily potent. If you cannot actually be present, try to be there spiritually. Public worship is more beneficial than private devotion.

Join small groups. Participate in the good things other Christians are trying to do. Cooperate with them even if you enjoy performing the same services as an individual. We glorify God through cooperative efforts to help others. Our presence at a church gathering can help everyone else.

God inspires us through his angels. They are also messengers from us to God. If you become acquainted with angels, you will begin to notice they are with you even though unseen. Those saints who have already left this world are "like the angels in heaven" (Matthew 22:30). They also inspire us and pray for us. In the same way that immature nightingales learn to sing by joining their voices with a group of older birds, the companionship of the saints will help us to pray better and to sing praise to God.

Give reverent attention to sermons. Apply the words you hear. Don't let them fall on the floor; take them into your heart. Keep a classic devotional book handy. I recommend Bonaventure, Teresa of Avila, Augustine's *Confession,* Scupoli's *Spiritual Combat,* Jerome's *Letters,* and similar books.

Inspiration

What do we mean when we say we are inspired? Inspiration is God's activity inside us. It could be a feeling of regret or an enlivening of interest. It is an increasing of desire to live the devout life. Anything that prompts us toward the divine is inspiration. It is like the Bridegroom in the Song of Songs waking up the bride and asking her to share his delights.

Marriage involves three steps before it is complete. It begins with a man's proposal, which is then accepted by the woman. Last, she is united with him. In a similar manner, God's proposal to us is inspiration. If we respond positively, we will then cooperate with God.

There are three steps to goodness: inspiration (the opposite of temptation), pleasure, and concurrence. It is not enough merely to be inspired. Until we take pleasure in it and act upon it, God is not satisfied. God attempted to get through to the Israelites for forty years after they escaped bondage in Egypt. "For forty years I was angry with that generation; I said, 'They are a people whose hearts go astray, and they have not known my ways.' So I declared on oath in my anger, 'They shall never enter my rest'" (Psalm 95:10-11).

Discovering pleasure in inspiration is a sign of spiritual progress. Your delight pleases God. Even though our agreement and participation do not yet fulfill it, it is still an unmistakable step in the right direction. Delighting in God's Word is an encouraging indicator of possibilities. The bride in the Song of Songs describes this kind of spiritual pleasure. "My heart had gone out to him when he spoke" (Song of Songs 5:6).

Consent is the only thing that fulfills good inspiration. Failing to respond positively is offensive to God. The bride delayed opening her door after she heard the Bridegroom's voice. "I looked for him but did not find him. I called him but he did not answer" (Song of Songs 5:6). She had missed an opportunity.

Philothea, let me give you one warning. There is a thin line between inspiration and temptation. When you feel inspired, listen calmly, lovingly, to the proposal. But before you give your consent regarding any significant or extraordinary divine suggestion, be certain to ask your spiritual director's opinion. It may be that the enemy has observed your receptive attitude and has taken advantage of his opportunity.

When you have given your consent to spiritually healthy inspiration, respond quickly. Acting upon it is the best thing you can do. It would be foolish to plant a grapevine without expecting it to yield fruit.

Confession

There is absolutely no reason to drain your spiritual energy with feelings of guilt. A lioness is quick to bathe herself after being close to a leopard. She does not want her mate to be disturbed by its scent. A soul that has sinned should be quickly cleansed to show respect to God. We are assured of God's pardon if we seek it.

A good time to admit sin is prior to Communion. Perhaps you can't think of anything really ugly in your experience. Use such a moment of confession to ask for the strength to resist future temptation and the ability to spot a temptation for what it is. With a little humility, the act of confession can become a multifaceted event of the greatest spiritual value.

Little sins deserve as much grief and attention as great sins. If you fail to seek the strength to change, you will remain encumbered by them even after confession. You will lose an opportunity to be free of them. Has your tongue been too busy? Do you waste time with trivial activities? Express your regret and announce your determination to do better. It is a blunder to confess any sin without sincerely desiring to be free of it.

Be specific when you confess your sins. Avoid generalities such as "I need to love God more" or "My prayers have not been profound" or "I have not loved my neighbor enough" or "I have been slack in my attendance at church." Anyone can say such things. It is more helpful to search for the reason behind such behavior. Why don't you love your neighbor? Is it because you turned away someone in need? Then go ahead and say so.

"I did not help that poor person even though it was within my ability. I turned away in selfish preoccupation." Confess with precision. If your prayer life is lackluster, express the reasons you think might contribute to this. Generalities in confession are "neither cold nor hot" (Revelation 3:15).

Look behind every sinful action for its motive. Suppose you told a lie. Why did you lie? Were you vainly trying to praise yourself or making an excuse? Admit if such sins have long been a part of your life. Have you been self-indulgent on a regular basis? Is it habitual? Name the sin. Examine the motive. Admit the span of time. This kind of confession will cleanse your soul, preparing it for the devout life.

Communion

King Mithridates of Pontus concocted an antidote to poisons. It is reported that he built up such a resistance that he was unable to commit suicide to avoid Roman slavery. Communion is our Lord's gift to us. "Here is the bread that comes down from heaven, which a man may eat and not die" (John 6:50). "Whoever eats my flesh and drinks my blood has eternal life" (John 6:54). Returning often to the table of our Lord strengthens and conditions the soul. We become resistant to the poisons of temptation and evil. We are so filled with the life-giving sacrament that spiritual death doesn't have a chance with us.

The tenderest fruits rot easily. Cherries, apricots, and strawberries, though, may easily be preserved with sugar and honey. Regardless of the weakness of our spirit, we can be spared spiritual decay when we ingest the bread and wine, the body and blood, of the Son of God.

Frequent Communion is commendable but not necessary. It seems to me that a devout person will want to participate at least monthly. If a friend asks why you are so diligent in attending the Lord's Supper, reply that you are trying to learn something about loving God. State that there are two kinds of people who need to commune regularly—the perfect and the imperfect. Acknowledge that you belong to the imperfect. You are like a sick patient visiting a doctor. Report that you regularly take Communion because you want to discover how to take it well. Everything takes practice.

Pliny writes that mountain rabbits have white fur in winter because all they can see and eat is snow. If you will feast upon the attractiveness, cleanliness, and goodness of God, you will also become attractive, clean, and good.

The Challenge of Christian Living

The queen bee is always accompanied by a group of lesser bees. In the same way, love comes to a person in concert with a host of many other virtues. Love is like an officer who commands an army, calling upon various units as the need arises. We become "like a tree planted by streams of water, which yields its fruit in season" (Psalm 1:3). Love irrigates the soul, causing it to bear the fruit of good behavior at the proper time. Such fruit comes in great variety and not all at the same time. The perfect thing to do on one occasion may be completely out of place on another. It is a mistake to think that you must always do a certain good thing all the time. One must not laugh or cry constantly. It is even more detrimental to look down on anyone who does not exhibit the same personality and preferences as your own. "Rejoice with those who rejoice; mourn with those who mourn" (Romans 12:15). "Love is patient, love is kind" (1 Corinthians 13:4). Love is unselfish, tactful, circumspect, and thoughtful.

While we may not be required to practice courage, altruism, and great self-sacrifice in many circumstances, we are constantly called upon to exhibit mildness, restraint, honesty, and humility. Such virtues as these are always in demand. They affect everything we do. We may prefer sugar, but salt is used more frequently. We need a good stock of the basic virtues.

What is required of one person may be different from that expected of another. A bishop needs certain qualities, a prince or a soldier needs others. All of us need all the virtues, but they are necessarily distributed unevenly. The specific assignment for each individual requires more of some and less of others.

Some virtues are more admirable and some are more visible. Comets appear to be larger than stars. In fact, they are vastly inferior to the stars. Comets are impressive because they are nearer to our eyes and are composed of disintegrating material. People tend to approve the most obvious virtues. It takes no special effort to discern them. Such virtues can almost be touched and tabulated. Almsgiving can be physical or spiritual. Material devices such as hair shirts, not wearing shoes, fasting and other deprivations of the body appeal to many. Meekness, gentleness, unpretentiousness, and other humblings of the heart are more difficult to observe, but they are superior virtues. Prefer the best rather than the most popular, Philothea. Impressive virtues may not be the best virtues.

It can be worthwhile to accent a certain virtue in your own life. This does not mean you disregard the others, but you should emphasize the application of one in order to focus your mind. Saint Francis of Assisi preferred poverty, calling his favorite "Lady Poverty." Saint Dominic enjoyed preaching. Saint Gregory the Great offered hospitality to travelers. Tobias put his love into practice by digging graves. Saint Catherine of Genoa became a hospital worker.

John Cassian, in his book, reports that a devout woman who had a desire to be more patient was given a special assignment by Saint Athanasius. He sent her to take care of an extremely unpleasant widow who was bitter, complaining, and impossible to please. She continually berated the devout woman. This produced many opportunities for the practice of loving patience.

God's workers, therefore, perform a wide variety of services with dedication to their particular task. In this way they select the material upon which they will embroider all Christian virtues. By relating the many virtues to the one preferred, they unify the individual virtues.

One way to overcome temptation is to immerse yourself in the virtue that is the complete opposite of the alluring vice, while calling upon all Christian virtues for support. This will not only defeat your soul's foe, it will also strengthen your character. If conceit or exasperation overtakes me, it is important for me to practice humility or gentleness quickly. The wild boar sharpens his tusks by grinding them against his other teeth. The result is that all his teeth are sharpened. A Christian can improve every area of character by using all virtues to help sharpen the one virtue that is particularly important in the present circumstance. Improving one improves them all.

Saint Augustine is correct when he tells us we naturally make certain mistakes when we begin the spiritual life. We want to get it right. We are overly concerned about each detail. This is entirely excusable. It is actually an indicator of promise for the future. On the other hand, anxiety about correctness and excessive attention to detail is not attractive in one who is experienced in devotion. Over time, love gradually overcomes such apprehensions.

When Bernard of Clairvaux began his work, he was extremely strict with his novices. He insisted they ignore the needs of the flesh and turn away from material things. He wanted them to give undivided attention to the soul. This harsh early guidance disheartened them. It required too much of beginners.

Bernard's own passionate spirit motivated him. He was eager to share his enthusiasm for the spiritual life. Unfortunately, his method did not produce the results he desired. God changed Bernard's demeanor. He gave him a spirit of humility and gentle warmth. He became compassionate and understanding. He could say with Paul, "To the weak I became weak, to win the weak. I have become all things to all men so that by all possible means I might save some" (1 Corinthians 9:22).

Paula, the daughter of Saint Jerome, overdid mortifications of the flesh. She could not be talked out of it. Her mourning for those who died was excessive enough to threaten her own health. Jerome was critical of her, saying she had perverted good behavior by taking it to extreme.

When a sick person's legs swell, it is taken as a good sign of getting well. The body is discharging extraneous fluid. If a person who is well has the same symptoms, it is an indication of trouble. Let's try to be understanding of anyone who fails while trying to get it right. The saints are often imperfect perfectionists. Then let's be careful in our own behavior and pay attention to our director's advice.

Some things people consider virtuous are not. I am thinking of ecstasies, rapturous insensibility, levitations, and similar magical stunts, which are proffered as the highest spiritual experiences. Philothea, if these things happen they are not virtues. They are nothing more than gifts from God. It is not right for us to seek them. They are irrelevant to loving and serving God. If they come, they come from outside us. All we are to try for is being good, devout men and women. If it pleases God to grant us a moment of angelic perfection, then we shall be good angels. But in the meantime, let's live sincerely, humbly, and devoutly. Let's live patiently, obediently, with tenderness toward our neighbors. Let's learn to put up with their imperfections. Let's desire no chief seats with God, but be glad to serve him in his kitchen or his pantry, to be his janitors or garbage-men. If later he wants us to serve on his private cabinet, so be it. But God does not reward his servants in relation to the dignity of their positions, but rather in relation to the love and humility they bring to their assigned tasks.

Frankly, ecstatic religious experience is highly subject to make-believe, artificial pretensions. Many who think they are angels are not even good people. They talk higher than they live. If you are awestruck by another's holiness, remain content with your own lower and safer experience. While it may not be spectacular, it is certainly appropriate for you. Humbly accept your own religious experience. God will pour out blessings on you.

PRACTICING TRUE PATIENCE

"You need to persevere so that when you have done the will of God, you will receive what he has promised" (Hebrews 10:36). Our Savior said, "By standing firm you will gain life" (Luke 21:19). Our Lord's torment and endurance saved us. We are called upon to endure hardship, injury, and difficulties with Christlike patience.

We cannot be selective about this, picking and choosing which slights and discomforts we will hold out against. Our patience is not to be reserved for only certain kinds of circumstances, but it must be applied to everything that comes our way. Some only want to suffer when it brings them honor. They are wounded in combat or suffer religious persecution. We are to endure patiently even when we are being dishonored.

To be picked on and criticized by mean people is of little concern to a courageous person. But to be denounced and treated badly by good people, by our own friends and relatives, is a true test of virtue. The sting of a bee is more painful than the bite of a fly. A distressing criticism from a good person can be hard to take. Sometimes two equally good people, both with good intentions, have ideas that conflict. They sometimes end up attacking each other and slinging mud. The jibes they exchange bring an injury that each must bear with patience.

Patience is also required when we deal with the attendant difficulties that come with a larger affliction. We are often more willing to accept a great pain than to cope with the accompanying irritations. "Poverty wouldn't bother me if it didn't prevent me from educating my children, helping others, and living respectfully." "I would not be upset by my present circumstance if it were clear that I am not responsible for it." "I do not care what evil is said about me as long as no one believes it." "I don't mind being sick, but I hate to be a bother."

Philothea, it is our job to be patient with the difficulty in all its fullness and not simply with a part of it. It is not simply a matter, say, of being sick, but of having this particular illness, right now, among these people, and with whatever side effects that may accompany it. Identical patience applies to every situation.

Accept any treatment and support you can. Then wait patiently to see what God will do. If God wills that you have relief, thank him. If the situation does not improve, patiently bless God.

If you deserve the criticism you receive, honestly admit it. If you are the target of an unjust accusation, politely deny your guilt. You owe it to both truth and your neighbor. If you continue to be accused after you have made a true and legitimate explanation, don't let that bother you.

There is no need to try to force anyone to agree with your explanation. Let it go. You have reported the facts, now be quiet.

Try not to complain about the things that irritate you. We often feel the problems we have are greater than those of others. Most important, never complain to someone who is quick-tempered and cranky. If you absolutely must protest to someone in order to correct an offense or to recover your peace of mind, then find a calm person who really loves God, for the hot-tempered person, instead of helping your situation, will stir up even more trouble. Instead of pulling the thorn out of your foot, that person will drive it in even deeper.

There is a false kind of patience that looks for emotional support from others. The sufferer wants to be seen as enduring great trials without bitterness. They manage to evoke sympathy without seeming to care for it. They are clever manipulators. "He had something to boast about—but not before God" (Romans 4:2).

The truly patient person neither whines nor seeks pity. If that person must speak of his sufferings, he will use a normal tone of voice and not exaggerate. If that person is extended pity for something he does not suffer, he will not accept it. This way he keeps peace between truth and patience.

When you encounter problems practicing the devout life, keep our Lord's words in your mind. "A woman giving birth to a child has pain because her time has come; but when her baby is born she forgets the anguish because of her joy that a child is born into the world. So with you: Now is your time of grief, but I will see you again and you will rejoice, and no one will take away your joy" (John 16:21-22). You have Jesus Christ within your soul. Take heart! These sorrows will pass and joy will remain with you.

During a time of illness, turn your distress, pain, and frailty over to our Lord. Ask if they can be of service to him. Ask if your suffering can be united with his. Follow your doctor's instructions, swallow your medicine, and accept any indignities in God's love. Recall the bitter cup he drank because he loves you. Let a desire to be of service to him motivate you to be well, but do not insist on good health. It may be that God wants to prepare you for death with an experience of illness. Honeybees make sweet honey from bitter nectar. There are few opportunities that allow us to do beautiful things and produce spiritual honey better than when we are eating the bitter food of sickness. Excellent honey is derived from small, harsh thyme flowers. Virtue practiced in a sickbed can be the best of all.

Reflect often upon the suffering of Jesus Christ. He was shaken by unimaginable weariness and sorrow, crucified, stripped naked, cursed, slandered, and forsaken. Your sufferings can in no way be compared with his. It is not possible for you to suffer for him as much as he has suffered for you. Are you asked to suffer as much as the martyrs? Are there not many who have it far worse than you?

EMBRACING HUMILITY

Elisha gave these instructions to a widow who was in great need: "Ask all your neighbors for empty jars. Don't ask for just a few. Then go inside and shut the door behind you.... Pour oil into all the jars" (2 Kings 4:3-4). Emptiness is a prerequisite for receiving gifts from God. We have to get ourselves out of the way. The kestrel has an expression and a cry that scare away hawks and other predacious birds. Doves prefer to live near the kestrel because this affords them security. Humility is similar to the kestrel. It keeps Satan at bay and protects the effects of God's grace within us. The most advanced in the devout life prize the virtue of humility above all others. It is clearly evident in Jesus and his mother.

Vanity is often inherited. It indicates that there is something about us that is not really ours. There is no true glory in being a descendent of nobility, of having important contacts, or being popular. People can become proud and arrogant because they ride a handsome horse or have a feather in their hat or wear well-tailored clothes. If there is any glory in such things it surely belongs to the horse, the bird, and the tailor! Others are proud of their mustache, hair, bodies, or their ability to dance, play cards, or sing. This is utter frivolity. Others want to be respected because of their education, as though they automatically become everyone's teacher.

You can spot genuine goodness the same way you can identify the best balm. If it sinks to the bottom of a container of water and stays there, it is the most valuable balm. Truly wise, learned, generous, noble persons will tend to be humble, modest, and eager to help others. If they float on the surface and show off, they are phonies. They are less genuine in direct proportion to their personal display.

Honors, titles, and rank are like saffron. Saffron grows best when it gets walked on. Being attractive is nice, but there is no honor in it if we are proud of it. Graceful beauty is natural and not cosmetic. Education brings no honor when it turns us into snobbish bores. Being fussy about position and rank has a way of exposing our ugliness. Honor is excellent when it is freely given to us by others, but it becomes cheap and degrading when we go looking for it. The peacock enjoys spreading his gorgeous tail feathers, but in the process he ruffles his other feathers in a most unattractive way. Beautiful flowers wither when plucked.

Intelligent people understand the pettiness of position, praise, and titles. They are occupied with more important things. The owner of pearls pays no attention to shells. The trinkets of society do not distract anyone who wants to be virtuous. One's position need not affect one's humility. An important person need not insist on favors and deference. Those who have visited Peru return with gold and silver, but they also bring monkeys and parrots. Monkeys and parrots are cheap and easy to transport. In the same way, those living the devout life can possess rank and position as long as it does not become burdensome. The exception would be when one is involved in a formal state occasion. Even then, the formalities can be tempered with kindly courtesy.

Some religious people are bothered by the possibility that they may be displaying God-given humility to receive recognition and praise. There is no way God's mercy and gifts to us can cause us to be proud. An awareness of what God has done for us will increase our humility. We are not responsible for anything good that is in us. Put the valuable, fragrant baggage of a prince on the back of a mule, and the mule is still a mule. Is there anything good about us that we did not receive as a gift? Why should it make us feel superior? Instead, our gratitude produces humility. Simply recall how life was before God mercifully came to you. That is what you can do on your own. Are you proud of it? Give God the credit for what you have been given and let all the praise be directed to him. "My soul glorifies the Lord and my spirit rejoices in God my Savior, for he has been mindful of the humble state of his servant" (Luke 1:46-47).

On the other hand, Philothea, don't make a pretense of being humble. My advice is that you should never talk about it, and by all means never ask to be given the lowest place if you only mean to start there and work your way to the top.

It is completely acceptable to be polite. Do not hesitate to offer someone an opportunity to step in front of you in line even if you know she will probably decline. This is not insincerity. It is good manners. The same is true regarding certain words we speak in polite conversation. They may not be technically accurate, but they are a part of standard greetings and exchanges. Be as honest as possible, but practice conventional courtesies.

Some people hold back in their spiritual life because they feel inadequate. For instance, they explain their failure to practice silent prayer on the grounds that they are not perfect enough. They do not participate in Communion because they feel unclean and poorly prepared. Some will not do the things they can do well for God and neighbor because they fear it may fill them with pride.

This is not the product of humility. It is a spiritual illness with nasty results. Such people are actually denigrating Christian behavior. They are attempting to secretly protect their own selfish notions and laziness. Their humility is a falsely applied thin veneer of deceit. It is a sham.

King Ahaz, for example, was given a wide-open opportunity. "The LORD spoke to Ahaz, 'Ask the LORD your God for a sign, whether in the deepest depths or in the highest heights.' But Ahaz said, 'I will not ask; I will not put the LORD to the test'" (Isaiah 7:10-12). He sidesteps an important spiritual opportunity with a pretense of humility. He fails to understand that our pride blocks God's desire to give us something valuable for our soul. True humility accepts what God is offering. We are obligated to take what God wants us to have. Humility admits we are not sufficient in ourselves and need God's help.

Consider knowledge in relation to humility. It is foolishness to think we know more than we actually do. Pretending to be better informed than we actually are is reprehensible egotism. I will not attempt to impress others with my education, but neither will I deny I know anything. Love sometimes requires us to share what we know in order to assist others. Humility sometimes hides and sometimes discloses. It both preserves and employs. It is like a tree that grows on Tylos Island. Its lovely blossoms close at night and open in the morning. Those who live there say the tree sleeps. Humility controls our virtues in the same manner. Usually they are hidden. For special needs, love instructs our humility to exhibit them.

We are asked to appear neither wise nor foolish. It is not a question of one or the other. You may discover that a few of God's great servants behaved oddly to make themselves appear less rational than they were. They had good reasons for doing this. You can respect them, but you are not in their unique circumstances. There is no reason for you to attempt to imitate them.

"As the ark of the LORD was entering the City of David, Michal daughter of Saul watched from a window. And when she saw King David leaping and dancing before the LORD, she despised him in her heart" (2 Samuel 6:16). David was not trying to look like a fool. He was giving expression to the overwhelming joy he felt on that great occasion. "When David returned home to bless his household, Michal daughter of Saul came out to meet him and said, 'How the king of Israel has distinguished himself today, disrobing in the sight of the slave girls of his servants as any vulgar fellow would!' David said to Michal, 'It was before the LORD, who chose me rather than your father or anyone from his house when he appointed me ruler over the LORD's people Israel—I will celebrate before the LORD. I will become even more undignified than this, and I will be humiliated in my own eyes'" (2 Samuel 6:20-22).

The Latin words for *humility* and *abjection* are synonymous. *Humility* means "abjection," and *abjection* means "humility." Mary's *Magnificat* includes the line, "He has been mindful of the humble state of his servant. From now on all generations will call me blessed" (Luke 1:48). Her point is that her Lord has observed her ordinariness. She is a common person without recognition or position of honor in the world. He uses her abject state as a way of giving her a great blessing.

Despite the close relationship of the two terms, there is a significant difference between *abjection* and *humility. Abjection* is a given condition that we do not always recognize. *Humility* is an admission that we perceive and acknowledge our lowliness. Moreover, with humility we can even rejoice in it. The most spiritually profitable abjection is not of our own choosing. We accept what God has given. God knows best.

You may consider the things I am saying to be difficult and painful to practice. This is not true. Once you begin to live the devout life, you will find it to be extraordinarily pleasant.

Humility prevents conceit. As a result, we will not go looking for applause and honor. At the same time, humility would not argue with the counsel of the wise man who said, "Have regard for your name, since it will outlive you longer than a thousand hoards of gold" (Sirach 41:12, NRSV). Caring about your reputation simply gives high regard to common morality and integrity. Humility permits us to recognize and value these things in ourselves. A good name is useful in civilized society. Love requires it. Humility concurs. We need to take care of our reputation.

A good reputation is something like leaves on a tree. Leaves are not particularly valuable in themselves, but they provide necessary services. They give the tree beauty, and they protect developing fruit from sunscald. A good reputation has little importance in itself, but it is attractive and protects developing virtues. Living up to what others think of us is a positive motivation.

Christians who are too sensitive about their good names and reputation are like those who take medicine for a slight indisposition. They think they are taking care of their health, but they are ruining it. When we are overly protective of our reputation, we may lose it completely. This is because our tenderness makes us argumentative and unbearable. This provokes our detractors even more.

Ignoring a negative comment about yourself is a better remedy than becoming resentful and planning revenge. Contempt for injuries makes them vanish. If we become angry we tacitly admit the truth of the accusation. Fear of losing our good name is the result of not trusting its foundation—a good life. Souls firmly anchored on Christian virtue can pay little attention to the torrent of a critical tongue.

Reputation is like a sign. It points to virtue. If your reputation is taken away by wagging tongues, don't be disturbed. Like a beard, it will grow out again. If God permits it to be taken from us, he will either give us a better one or help us with holy humility.

I would make only a few exceptions. If the unjust accusation refers to horrible crimes, no one should be expected to put up with it. Let the accused justly acquit himself of it. Additionally, if an individual needs a spotless reputation in order to help others, that person should quietly seek a correction.

CONTROLLING ANGER

Our Lord said, "Learn from me; for I am gentle and humble in heart" (Matthew 11:29). Humility affects our relationship with God; gentleness involves our neighbor. Earlier I noted that the best balm (representing humility) sinks to the bottom while oil (representing gentleness) rises to the top. This meekness is the like the topmost flower in a good arrangement. Gentleness is a supreme Christian virtue.

When Joseph was in Egypt, his brothers visited with him during a time of famine. "Then he sent his brothers away, and as they were leaving he said to them, 'Don't quarrel on the way!'" (Genesis 45:24). The same advice applies to us, Philothea. The life we live on earth is a journey to another life. It is not good for us to be angry with each other as we travel. We need to be unified as a family. Let us be good company, held together with gentleness, harmony, and love. Let me be blunt about it: Don't get angry. As far as it is possible, never let it happen. Do not allow anger to get its foot in the door to your heart. "Everyone should be quick to listen, slow to speak and slow to become angry, for man's anger does not bring about the righteous life that God desires" (James 1:19-20).

Sometimes it is necessary to correct others. It is our duty to be courageous and take such action, but let it be done peacefully and gently. A raging elephant is calmed when it sees a little lamb. Soft wool gently cushions the blow of a cannonball. Hotheaded commands do little to correct behavior. A reasonable person responds to reasonable instruction. Only tyranny can enforce passionate control. Reason is not at home with passion. A royal visit brings pleasure to a community when it is peaceful. If such a visit is associated with armies and war, it is harmful and undesirable even if it is intended to be beneficial. Reason does not need to be accompanied with rage. Serious correction can be applied without becoming angry or hostile. "Do not let the sun go down while you are still angry" (Ephesians 4:26). If we remain angry when night comes, it will become hatred. Hatred is even more difficult to control than anger. It feeds on many incorrect ideas. No angry person ever thinks the anger is unjustified.

Try to live without anger. This is better than even a careful, controlled application of it. When we do something that upsets us, we need to stop our rage immediately. If we allow even a little of it to rise within us, it will take over. It is like the snake that can pull its entire length into any place it can put its head.

You ask me how it is possible to control your natural anger. Your response to your own anger, Philothea, should be calm and gentle while being firm and intense. A violent response to one's anger is counterproductive. During a heavy debate in a crowded senate chamber or parliament, a sergeant at arms may start yelling, "Order! Be quiet!" He becomes louder than the ones who are arguing. It is possible to overexcite yourself while attempting to control your anger.

Let God help you with your anger. Turn to him and pray, "Hear, O LORD, and be merciful to me; O LORD, be my help" (Psalm 30:10). When the apostles were caught in a storm at sea, they woke Jesus and said to him, "Lord, save us! We're going to drown!" (Matthew 8:25). He took control of the situation and calmed the wind and the waves. He will do the same with your emotions. He will bring a great calm to you. The prayers you make under duress may be spoken calmly and without being disturbed.

One more thing is important. The moment you take any rash action or speak a harsh word, take it back. Instantly correct yourself. The best cure for telling lies is to tell the truth immediately. Fresh injuries heal the fastest. Promptly follow any outburst of anger with an expression of regret and a correcting action.

During peaceful times, fill your storehouse with gentleness and kindness. Speak and behave in the nicest way you can. Be courteous not only with strangers, but also with those nearest you. Some appear to be angels in public but are devils at home.

BALANCING SELF-REPROACH

Don't dwell upon your lack of perfection. It is natural to be sorry when we recognize we have made a poor choice, but there is no value in harsh, dismal, rancorous, and emotional disapproval of yourself. It is easy to fall into this trap. If we yield to a moment of anger, we then become angry with ourselves for being angry. We are bothered because we have allowed ourselves to be bothered. This kind of response keeps emotional tension high.

The second annoyance does not correct the first. It makes us even more irritable. Worst of all, we can even become proud that we are denigrating ourselves. We can actually enjoy admitting our limitations.

Yes, let's acknowledge our flaws and regret them. But let's do that in a calm, unemotional way. A judge who is not emotionally involved in the case before him will render a more rational judgment. He will recognize the facts of a crime and not be misled by what it may seem to be. We can be unfair in our self-reproach. We may have a distorted view of what's important, giving excessive attention to one area of behavior and ignoring others. Conscience is more often dictated by emotion than by reason.

A parent does a much better job of correcting a child with gentle guidance rather than screaming rage. It works the same way when we correct ourselves. Compassion is superior to passion. Rebuke yourself gently. The results will reach deeper into your soul.

If I have determined to avoid being vain and still succumb to it, I would *not* say to myself, "You have failed. After all your good resolutions you have done the thing you meant to avoid. Shame on you. How can you ever pray again? You are a traitor, rebelling against God." Instead, I would attempt to be more understanding of myself. "Well, here I am. I went against my own wishes. I did the very thing I promised myself I did not want to do. There is nothing to be gained by staying here. Get out of this trap. Ask for God's mercy. Let God direct you in the future. Begin again. Cheer up now, and be more careful next time. God will bring improvement." This approach will give me a solid foundation for building stronger resistance against that particular failure.

Some personalities may require a firmer reproach than this. If you must be rougher on yourself, don't drag it out. Be done with it. Then repeat the psalm: "Why are you downcast, O my soul? Why so disturbed within me? Put your hope in God, for I will yet praise him, my Savior and my God" (Psalm 43:5). Trust God's mercy. Start over again, more determined than ever.

CARING WITHOUT WORRYING

Being concerned does not require anxiety. Pay careful attention to whatever God has put in front of you, but don't fret over it. Worry interferes with clear thinking. It will induce us to make a mess of the very thing we are fretting over. Recall our Lord's visit to Mary and Martha. "Martha was distracted by all the preparations that had to be made. She came to him and asked, 'Lord, don't you care that my sister has left me to do the work by myself? Tell her to help me!' 'Martha, Martha,' the Lord answered, 'you are worried and upset about many things, but only one thing is needed'" (Luke 10:40-42). She was taking the situation too seriously, overestimating the importance of every detail. Rivers that have a gentle, steady current can move great barges that are loaded with goods. Gentle showers irrigate huge farms. Deluge and flood are destructive. Do something hastily, and it will be sloppy work. "It is not good to have zeal without knowledge, nor to be hasty and miss the way" (Proverbs 19:2). A job done well is completed soon enough. Drones are noisy bees, but they make wax rather than honey. People who make a big fuss over their assignment produce little, and the results are often inferior.

It is possible to get lost in the details. Flies are not a bother because they are strong, but because there are so many of them. Serious business is not nearly as troubling as trivial details. Take it one step at a time. If it is a complicated task, there is no way you can do it all at once. You will feel overwhelmed. Organize it. Then you will make steady, deliberate progress without getting excited.

Trust God's providence, but cooperate with him. Be like a little child who holds his father's hand while picking strawberries or blackberries in the hedgerows. If you must deal with the world's commerce with one hand, keep the other one with God. Look up to him now and then to see if he approves of what you are doing. Never think that you will be able to gather more if you use both hands. He is your success. Let go of him and you are in peril.

What I am getting at, Philothea, is that if your business is common enough, look at God rather than at it. If it becomes complicated and demands all of your attention, then still look now and then at God, the way sailors look at the sky rather than the water. This way God will work with you, in you, and for you.

THE FREEDOM OF SPIRITUAL POVERTY

"Blessed are the poor in spirit, for theirs is the kingdom of heaven" (Matthew 5:3). This is the opposite of having an obsession with wealth. A kingfisher's nest is shaped like an apple. Built at the ocean's edge, it has only a small entrance on top. It is skillfully designed to withstand splashing waves, maintaining a dry interior. The nest is always close to water, but it is not endangered by it. Philothea, your heart should also be open only to heaven above. It needs to be watertight, resistant to the passing things of this world. Regardless of how much you accumulate, do not become attached to your possessions. Even if you are in a sea of riches, you do not need to be in love with riches. Do not let material things become your master. Keep your spirit free of the things that decay. Remain independent of your wealth. This makes it possible for you to have all the advantages of wealth without sacrificing spiritual poverty.

There is a big difference between having poison and taking poison. Pharmacists keep all kinds of poisons on their shelves. They are not harmed because it is only in their shop and not in themselves. You can have great wealth without being harmed by it. All you have to do is keep it in your home and your purse rather than in your heart.

We do not easily admit that we are greedy. Most people would deny this. Perhaps we excuse ourselves by saying we have to take care of our children. Prudence is an obligation. But then we can never have too much. We always need more. Greed is extremely hard to detect, but it is insatiable.

Try this test for yourself. Do you really crave something enough to do something crooked to get it? Will your desires deprive another of his possessions? "There was an incident involving a vineyard belonging to Naboth.... The vineyard was in Jezreel, close to the palace of Ahab king of Samaria. Ahab said to Naboth, 'Let me have your vineyard to use for a vegetable garden, since it is close to my palace. In exchange I will give you a better vineyard or, if you prefer, I will pay you whatever it is worth.'

"But Naboth replied, 'The LORD forbid that I should give you the inheritance of my fathers.'

"So Ahab went home, sullen and angry.... He lay on his bed sulking and refused to eat" (1 Kings 21:1-4).

Ahab was prepared to do honest business, but Naboth had very good justification for declining the offer. The greatest right to something material belongs to the one who already owns it. It is soon enough to desire your neighbor's property when he is ready to get rid of it.

If you are strongly attached to the things you own, you will worry a lot about losing them. When people who are feverish are given a glass of water, they drink it with an eagerness and satisfaction that you don't often see in a healthy person. If you find yourself destroyed by a loss of property, you love it too much. The clearest proof of love for a lost object is suffering because it is lost.

Don't desire wealth you do not have. Don't attach your heart too closely to what you already have. Shed no tear for your losses. If you can do this, it is possible that even if you are rich, you are also poor in spirit and the kingdom of heaven is yours.

The gardeners who maintain royal estates take better care of them than they would their own property. Why? Because they want to please their bosses.

Our possessions are not our own. God has put them in our care. He wants us to cultivate them and make them fruitful enough to turn a profit. Our job is to take good care of what has been entrusted to us.

Those who do not realize this are laboring only out of selfishness. This ignorance can cause a violent struggle. There is always a sense of uneasiness and impending danger. If we are working for God, life is much more calm and peaceful. Let's be careful to remember this as we preserve and increase our material possessions.

Be on the lookout for avarice. Make it a habit to give away some of what you have. Give it with a generous heart. Nothing makes us more prosperous than to give alms to the poor. Any poverty brought on by giving alms is holy and rich.

Love poverty and love those who are poor. This is the way to really become poor yourself. We become like what we love. Love is the great equalizer. Paul asks, "Who is weak, and I do not feel weak?" (2 Corinthians 11:29). We could easily paraphrase him this way: "Who is poor and I am not also poor?" Love gives him kinship with the ones he loves. Love the poor and you will join them in their poverty. Visit them regularly. Welcome them as guests at your home. Enjoy conversations with them. Sit beside them in church. Walk with them. Be one of them even as you help them out of your position of wealth.

Don't stop with merely giving possessions away. Make yourself the servant of the poor. Go to them and wait on them when they are sick in bed. Wait on them with your own hands. Prepare their food for them at your own expense. Do their laundry. Such service is more glorious than working for a king.

Saint Louis was among the greatest kings of all time. He regularly served the poor and had them join him for meals. He would often dine on their leftovers. During his frequent hospital visits, he was known to wait upon lepers and those with disgusting sores. He rendered these services bareheaded while kneeling on the ground beside the sick person. He loved them and cared for them as tenderly as a mother would tend her sick child.

This kind of poverty comes from the blessed who are a part of the kingdom of heaven. "Come, you who are blessed by my Father; take your inheritance, the kingdom prepared for you since the creation of the world. For I was hungry and you gave me something to eat, I was thirsty and you gave me something to drink, I was a stranger and you invited me in, I needed clothes and you clothed me, I was sick and you looked after me, I was in prison and you came to visit me" (Matthew 25:34-36). That is what the King of the poor and the King of kings will announce on Judgment Day.

Most of us experience inconveniences. Perhaps a guest visits us, but we lack the means to entertain that guest. Or maybe we need to appear in public, but our good clothes are somewhere else. What if the wine in our cellar turns sour? Or when traveling, we have to spend a night in a cheap hotel? It is easy to lack something, no matter how rich we are. Rejoice in such occasions. Accept them with a good and cheerful heart.

If you lose something to fire, flood, wind, drought, theft, or lawsuits, it is time to practice a little spiritual poverty. Accept your losses meekly and patiently. Be courageous in submitting to such impoverishment.

Esau had natural hair on his arms. Jacob did not. Jacob wore hairy gloves to trick his nearly blind father. If anyone had pulled the hair off of Jacob's arms, he would not have felt it. Esau would have screamed with pain, become angry, and defended himself. Because our possessions stick in our hearts, we complain loudly when natural catastrophes and crime take them from us. But if we think of our possessions only as something lent from God, we won't go crazy when they are taken from us.

Spiritual Wealth When You Are Really Poor

You can turn unavoidable poverty into something valuable. It can be like a priceless jewel that is invisible to the worldly minded. Accept poverty graciously. It puts you in some very good company. Our Lord was poor, as were his mother and his disciples. Many of the saints were poor. Some had the opportunity to be rich but consciously decided to be poor instead. Many had to go to great bother to be rid of their wealth. If poverty has arrived at your door without any effort on your part, be glad. Welcome poverty as a close friend of Jesus Christ. He was born into it. He lived in it. He died in it. He was nurtured by poverty all his life.

Two privileges come with your poverty. Since you did not choose it, it is God's will and not your own. Anything we receive from God with gratitude is a great blessing. Unsought poverty must please God. When our own desire is not involved, the greatest degree of God's desire is expressed. A modest, uncomplaining acceptance of what God has selected for us purifies and refines our suffering.

The other privilege of unsought poverty is its honesty. Poverty that is acclaimed, fondled, respected, sustained, and tended is a companion of wealth. It does not have the wholeness of true poverty.

Since we naturally complain about things that are disagreeable to us, don't complain about your poverty. If you do, you are rich in desire rather than poor in spirit. To seek a poverty that does not bring along any difficulties is pointless. It is not possible to have both poverty's honor and wealth's advantages.

There is no shame in being poor or in asking for help. Graciously accept what is given you and do not become belligerent when you are denied. Remember Mary's hasty journey into Egypt for the protection of her son. Recall the suffering, destitution, and scorn she endured. Live this way and you will have a spiritually rich poverty.

HONEST FRIENDSHIP

Love is the soul's strongest passion. It is the most powerful motivator. We are controlled and shaped by what we love. We become like what we love. Be careful, Philothea, to love only what is good. If you love something that is corrupt, you will become corrupt.

Of all the loves, friendship brings the most risk. This is true because friendship involves interaction. Love is possible without friendship. We can love without being loved in return. Friendship is mutually shared. If it is not shared, it is not friendship. Both friends are conscious of their friendship. Like a communicable disease, we cannot communicate with another person without sharing the qualities of the message.

All friendships are not equal. Superb honey is collected from the most delightful flowers. Friendship that is based on the highest loves is also superior. A poisonous honey is produced at Heraclea in Pontus. The bees collect it from the flowers of the aconite that grow there. Anyone who eats that honey will become insane. Friendships can also be poisonous when they are based on incorrect and depraved grounds.

There is more to a good marriage relationship than physical pleasures. Animals are also attracted to each other. If the relationship is based entirely upon physical attraction, it is no higher than that of donkeys and horses. True friendship in marriage involves a sharing of life, labor, possessions, endearment, and continuing faithfulness. This is an honest, sacred friendship.

Young people tend to base their friendships on such things as a fine mustache or head of hair, smiling glances, well-tailored clothes, and knowledge of what's in fashion. This is acceptable for those who are still only in blossom and whose judgment is only in bud. These friendships are passing things. They melt like snow in the sun.

Sometimes people of the opposite sex have playful friendships without considering marriage. These are merely phantoms of friendship. They are not entitled to the name of either friendship or love.

Some people simply need to love or be loved. They give in to amorous desires. As soon as they meet someone who appeals to them, they begin fond communication. They do not even bother to examine the other person's character. They are caught in sordid nets and have a hard time getting themselves out of these entanglements. These relationships are a waste of time, a loss of honor, and satisfy nothing but an insatiable curiosity. People think they have a right to expect something from it all, but they are not sure what it is. In this game the one who catches is also caught. Can you feel sorry for the snake charmer who is bitten by a snake?

It is a terrible mistake to gamble away the greatest power of your soul for trivial things. God takes notice of your soul. Spiritually, it is your will that matters. The important thing about your will is its love. We dare not throw away love for valueless junk when we already lack enough love for God. An infinite God deserves our complete soul-love. We will need to report all deductions from our limited supply of love that we take for anything other than God.

A walnut tree is poisonous to other growing plants. Its roots make it very difficult for other things to live nearby. Its leaves cause dense shade. Its fruit attracts many who gather it, trampling tender seedlings. A fondness for anything other than God can have the same effect on your soul. Such diversions are playfulness among courtiers but a pestilence of the heart. (*Le jouet des cours, mais la peste des coeurs.*)

Love all people with a genuine love, but be friends only with a few who share your values. The higher your values are, the better the friendships will be. When you share religious love and Christian devotion, the resulting friendship will be a thing of beauty. Its excellence finds its source in God. It is outstanding because it also leads to God and will endure eternally. We can begin to love here in this life in the same way love is experienced in heaven.

This spiritual friendship is distinct from the love we have for all of God's children. This is a situation where a few people bond together in a shared devotion to God. With a unity of spirit and purpose it may be said of them, "It is truly wonderful when relatives live together in peace" (Psalm 133:1, CEV). Other friendships only hint at what is achieved here. They are held together with glass chains. These are bound with golden devotion. This is the only friendship worth establishing for yourself. Of course, you need to continue those friendships that naturally involve you with your parents, family, patrons, and neighbors.

There is a popular notion that we should avoid all friendships because they distract our attention and may lead to envy. This is not clear thinking. The rules and conditions that apply to the monastic life are not universally applicable. A monastery is a unique environment with mutually shared spiritual goals. Close friendships can actually become a distraction. Devout people who live in the ordinary world need vital association with others who share their devotion. They encourage and inspire each other. Those who walk on level ground have no need to offer or accept a hand. If they are climbing a rocky or slippery hill, they take hold of each other for security.

Members of religious orders travel a well-paved road. The rest of us pass through some rough and dangerous places. We need each other. There is no agreement among the variety of people in the world regarding what is good and holy. We travel our chosen path and seek companions who are in harmony with our purpose. This results in a degree of separation, but it is a holy separation. The only division it produces is a line between good and bad, between sheep and goats, between bees and hornets. Recognizing the difference is essential.

The Bible reports that Jesus had close friends. He often visited Mary, Martha, and Lazarus in Bethany. Peter was a good friend of Mark. Paul befriended Timothy. Saint Jerome, Saint Augustine, Saint Bernard, and many other outstanding servants of God had special friendships which in no way detracted from their spiritual perfection. One of Paul's complaints against pagans was that they were "heartless" (Romans 1:31). They did not establish honest friendships. Thomas Aquinas describes special friendships with a few people as a virtue. He says it is impossible to have such friendships with many. We may conclude that spiritual perfection does not come without close friends. Rather, it includes some really virtuous, holy, and sacred friendships.

Let me caution you, Philothea. I have already mentioned the poisonous honey that is produced in Heraclea. It looks like an excellent honey, but it is toxic. It is still dangerous even when it is mixed with other honey. This kind of deception is also a part of human friendships. There are great risks.

It is possible to determine the difference between the hazardous honey from Heraclea and wholesome honey. Heraclean honey has an exaggerated sweetness. This is because its source is sweet aconite. Secular friendships may drip with sweet words. A profusion of compliments, praise, and endearments are spoken. Sacred friendships do not need these excesses. Simple, plain language is sufficient. Any praise is given to God. Moreover, God is recognized as the very foundation upon which the friendship is established. "Those who fear the Lord direct their friendship aright" (Sirach 6:17, NRSV). On the contrary, "Don't you know that friendship with the world is hatred toward God? Anyone who chooses to be a friend of the world becomes an enemy of God" (James 4:4).

MORTIFICATION OF THE FLESH

Palladius, in his book on agriculture, indicates it may be possible to make an inscription on an almond seed, return it to its shell, bind it gently, and then plant it. The resulting tree, he says, will produce almonds bearing that same inscription.

It is a waste of time to try to improve a person by working on things like hair, clothes, and posture. It is better to begin improving things with the seed kernel on the inside. "'Even now,' declares the LORD, 'return to me with all your heart'" (Joel 2:12). "My son, give me your heart and let your eyes keep to my ways" (Proverbs 23:26). Our activities begin in our heart. As the heart is, so is our behavior. The divine Bridegroom gives this invitation to the soul, "Place me like a seal over your heart, like a seal over your arm" (Song of Songs 8:6). Anyone whose heart is familiar with Jesus Christ will quickly exhibit him in things said and done.

This is why I have wanted to inscribe *Live, Jesus!* on your heart, Philothea. It's something like marking that almond seed. With Jesus living in your heart, he will also live in your behavior and comments. You will be able to repeat Saint Paul's words, "I have been crucified with Christ and I no longer live, but Christ lives in me" (Galatians 2:20).

Here are some tips to help you prepare your heart for the divine presence. If fasting is not injurious for you, it would be worthwhile to fast a few days beyond those designated on the church calendar. There are results beyond those commonly reported. In addition to an uplifting of your spirit, limiting your body's tyranny, and increasing virtue, it will also take control of your appetite, subjecting it to spiritual law. Early Christians fasted on Wednesdays, Fridays, and Saturdays. You can fast on some of these days also. Follow your director's guidance on this.

I agree with Saint Jerome's comment to Leda that long, immoderate fasts, particularly among young people, are not good. They are counterproductive. Stags are not able to run well when they are too fat, and also when they are too lean. Our bodies will be a problem for us both when they are excessively pampered and when they are run down. We can't support them when they are obese, and they can't support us when they are too flimsy. Fast in moderation. Overdo it and you will not be of value to anyone. If you begin severely, you will turn to a softer life. It would be far better to engage in a sensibly balanced approach to fasting that permits you to continue to be of service to others.

After all, fasting and working are both able to subdue the flesh. Your business may add to God's glory. In my opinion, it is better to endure the ache of working than the ache of fasting. Keeping our bodies strong and healthy is superior to ruining your health and vitality. We can discipline our bodies whenever we wish, but we cannot restore good health as easily.

Our Savior told his disciples, "Eat what is set before you" (Luke 10:8). Take it as it comes. There is no advantage in seeking something worse than what is set before you. You may think such a choice is true austerity, but it is not. It takes far more discipline to accept whatever comes your way without expressing your personal taste. This effort requires us to put aside both our preference and our choice. There is no public display in this kind of self-control. Since it is entirely a personal thing, it does not interfere with social activities. Setting one food aside in order to receive something else, analyzing and criticizing how it is prepared, being difficult to please, and commenting upon every carefully examined mouthful is indicative of an insecure person who is obsessed with culinary delights and dainty dishes. "Eat what is set before you."

We may make an exception for unhealthy foods. It is best to avoid highly seasoned, gassy, stomach-upsetting dishes. It is not easy to work for God when your digestive system is out of order. Aim for a steady, sober moderation. This is much better than a time of radical fasting followed by overeating. Moderate discipline has a way of quickening spiritual awareness. Classical tools of self-punishment, such as the hair shirt, truly punish the flesh, but these are not acceptable for use by married or frail people. These are used on rare occasions in circumstances that are unique and controlled.

Nights are made for sleep. Individuals differ in their requirements for sleep. Be sure to get enough sleep each night to be able to function at full capacity during the day. Sleeping late robs you of the best part of the day. The Scriptures and the example of the saints confirm our suspicion that morning is the most valuable time. I recommend going to bed early in order to get up early. A clear, bright sunrise comes at the least disturbed time of the day. The birds help us wake up and sing praise to God. Starting the day early is profitable for both body and soul.

An Old Testament story makes a strong point. "Balaam got up in the morning, saddled his donkey and went with the princes of Moab. But God was very angry when he went, and the angel of the LORD stood in the road to oppose him.... When the donkey saw the angel of the LORD standing in the road with a drawn sword in his hand, she turned off the road into a field. Balaam beat her to get her back on the road.

"Then the angel of the LORD stood in a narrow path between two vineyards, with walls on both sides. When the donkey saw the angel of the LORD, she pressed close to the wall, crushing Balaam's foot against it. So he beat her again.

"Then the angel of the LORD moved on ahead and stood in a narrow place where there was no room to turn, either to the right or to the left. When the donkey saw the angel of the LORD, she lay down under Balaam, and he was angry and beat her with his staff. Then the LORD opened the donkey's mouth, and she said to Balaam, 'What have I done to you to make you beat me these three times?'

"Balaam answered the donkey, 'You have made a fool of me! If I had a sword in my hand, I would kill you right now.'

"The donkey said to Balaam, 'Am I not your own donkey, which you have always ridden, to this day? Have I been in the habit of doing this to you?'

"'No,' he said.

"Then the LORD opened Balaam's eyes, and he saw the angel of the LORD standing in the road with his sword drawn. So he bowed low and fell facedown.

"The angel of the LORD asked him, 'Why have you beaten your donkey these three times? I have come here to oppose you because your path is a reckless one before me. The donkey saw me and turned away from me these three times. If she had not turned away, I would certainly have killed you by now, but I would have spared her.'

"Balaam said to the angel of the LORD, 'I have sinned. I did not realize you were standing in the road to oppose me. Now if you are displeased, I will go back'" (Numbers 22:21-34).

The point is, Philothea, Balaam is his own problem, but he punishes the poor beast that has nothing to do with it.

We make the same mistake with religiously inspired self-punishment. When a woman has a sick husband or sick child, she may begin to fast or to wear a hair shirt. When you punish your body like this, you are merely beating the poor beast that carries you around. There is no way your body can remedy the situation. If God's sword is drawn against you, it is not your body's fault. There is nothing it can do to help you. Discipline your heart, your deepest desires, your sincerest beliefs. It may be filled with arrogance, conceit, and cravings.

Perhaps you are obsessed with a desire for sex. An encounter with someone may leave you remorseful if your heart regains control and brings you to your senses. Then you may begin to think, "My flesh has betrayed me. My wicked body has taken control of me." You determine the best thing to do is to punish your body. Perhaps you will stop eating. Maybe you will find a way to inflict pain. You engage in some sort of self-flagellation. If your body could talk like Balaam's donkey, it would say, "Hey! Why are you punishing me? God is displeased with your soul's choices, not with your body's activity. You are the guilty one. Why do you misuse my eyes, hands, and lips without restraint? Why do you stir me up with impure thoughts? Correct your thinking and I will cause you no problems. Avoid bad companions and I will not become aroused. You throw me into the fire and then ask me not to burn!"

What God desires of you is a repentant and changed heart. Washing your skin does not cleanse your blood. Purify your heart, your affections. Most important, never attempt any kind of physical rigor independent of the guidance and monitoring of your spiritual director.

SOLITUDE AND COMMUNITY LIFE

We are neither to seek nor to avoid exchanges with other people. If we do not wish to be with them, we reveal haughtiness and scorn. Jesus said, "Love your neighbor as yourself" (Matthew 22:39). Shunning a neighbor is hardly a way of demonstrating love. Similarly, if we really love ourselves we need to spend some time alone within ourselves.

If you are not under an obligation to mingle socially or entertain others in your home, remain within yourself. Entertain yourself. If visitors arrive or you are called out to someone for a good reason, go as one who is sent by God. Visit your neighbor with a loving heart and a good intention.

There is great risk in visiting mean and vicious people. Honeybees do not mingle with wasps and hornets. For us, it is something like exposure to rabies. As for ordinary social gatherings, we need to be neither too careful to participate in them nor impolite in condemning them. We can modestly do our duty.

Sometimes we make some pointless visits simply for a little distraction from more serious concerns. There is nothing wrong with these visits as long as they only fill leisure time. They are a form of recreation.

Certain devout souls you visit will greatly bless the time you spend with them. Get with them as often as you can, Philothea. There is much in such exchanges that will enhance your devotion. A grapevine planted among olive trees will produce grapes tainted with the taste of olives. A soul in the proximity of genuinely good people will not be able to escape the infusion of some of their fine qualities. Get closely acquainted with honestly devout people.

In all of your mixing with others, be natural, sincere, and modest. Some people annoy others with their affectations. Some don't speak; they sing instead. Some take steps and must count every one out loud to you. This becomes irritating. Artificiality in social life is very disagreeable.

A modest cheerfulness should be present in our conversations with others. Some of the saints have been highly praised because of their good cheer and sense of humor. The apostle Paul says, "Rejoice with those who rejoice" (Romans 12:15). He also says, "Rejoice in the Lord always. I will say it again: Rejoice! Let your gentleness be evident to all" (Philippians 4:4-5).

Rejoicing "in the Lord" has certain qualifications. Whatever you are enjoying must be both lawful and appropriate. Not everything that is legal is also proper. Many tasteless practical jokes fall into this category—tripping someone, splattering a face, teasing and taunting, making sport of a handicapped person.

In addition to a mental solitude to which you can retreat even in the middle of a crowd, learn to love actual physical solitude. There is no need to go out into the desert. Simply spend some quiet time alone in your room, in a garden, or some other place. There you can think some holy thoughts or do a little spiritual reading. One of the great bishops said, "I walk alone on the beach at sunset. I use such recreation to refresh myself and shake off a little of my ordinary troubles."

Our Lord received a glowing report from his apostles about how they had preached and what a great ministry they had done. Then he said to them, "Come with me by yourselves to a quiet place and get some rest" (Mark 6:31).

CLOTHING

Saint Paul gives devout women a directive regarding the choice of clothes. The same principle applies equally to men. "Dress modestly, with decency and propriety, not with braided hair or gold or pearls or expensive clothes" (1 Timothy 2:9). Wear clean clothes. In a way, a neat outward appearance is indicative of an orderly soul. God requires physical cleanliness of anyone who approaches his altar.

Clothing style is dictated by your circumstances. Certain clothes are more appropriate at some times and places than at others. Young people have more freedom to experiment with stylish clothes and ornamentation. Older people simply look ridiculous wearing youthful things.

Take care of your appearance, Philothea. Neatness shows respect for others. The thing to avoid is ostentatious and flamboyant attire. Keep it simple and modest. This is true beauty.

In my opinion, Christian men and women should be the best dressed but least conspicuous in any group of people.

OUR MANNER OF SPEAKING

Doctors sometimes learn about a person's health by looking at his tongue. The tongue can also be a guide to diagnosing the condition of the soul. "For by your words you will be acquitted, and by your words you will be condemned" (Matthew 12:37). Our hand quickly moves to the location of pain, and our tongue goes for what we like. Anyone genuinely in love with God will frequently speak of him in ordinary conversation. "The mouth of the righteous man utters wisdom, and his tongue speaks what is just" (Psalm 37:30).

In the same way that bees use their tiny tongues to extract nothing but honey, so your tongue should always be sweetened with God. There is no greater pleasure than to taste the praise of his holy name blossoming between your lips. It is reported that whenever Saint Francis of Assisi would speak the name of Jesus, he would lick his lips as though he wanted to gather something sweet.

Be careful! Always speak of God with reverence and devotion. This is not for showing off your religiosity. Speak in a spirit of humility and love. Distill your devotion's honey a little drop at a time into the ears of others. In the secret depths of your soul, ask God to be pleased with this holy dew you are passing into the heart of your listener. Above all else, speak with meekness and gentleness. It is not to be done for correction but for inspiration.

Never mention God or devotion in an ordinary or careless way. Be reverent and attentive. I am telling you this so that you might escape the strange vanity found in some who talk about devotion. They speak pious words mechanically, as though they were not aware of what they were saying. When they speak like this, they think they are in harmony with their words, but they are not.

"If anyone is never at fault in what he says, he is a perfect man" (James 3:2). Never let an indecent word slip from your mouth. Even if you don't mean it in an evil way, others may be offended. An evil word dropping into a weak person grows and spreads like a drop of oil on linen. It might spark a thousand unclean thoughts and temptations. If bodily poison enters through the mouth, spiritual poison enters through the ear. The tongue that does the speaking is a murderer of a soul.

Don't try to tell me you speak without thinking. Our Lord who searches our hearts says, "Out of the overflow of the heart the mouth speaks" (Matthew 12:34). Even if it is not our intention to do any harm, our words may still damage the one who listens. Those who eat an herb called *angelica* have sweet breath. Those who have angelic virtues within their hearts speak sweetly.

As for profanity and obscenity, the apostle Paul doesn't even want us to be familiar with such language: "Among you there must not be even a hint of sexual immorality, or of any kind of impurity, or of greed, because these are improper for God's holy people" (Ephesians 5:3). He insists that "bad company corrupts good character" (1 Corinthians 15:33).

Indecent words that are interjected with subtlety are even more damaging. A sharp dart penetrates most easily. The more pointed an obscenity, the deeper it penetrates the heart. Those who proudly imagine they are sophisticated do not fully understand what conversation is when they use such words. Rather than being honey-gathering bees, they are wasps out to sting. Turn away from anyone who speaks to you in a bawdy manner.

Scoffing at others is a wretched practice. God detests this vice. In the Old Testament he inflicts unusual punishments on scoffers. There can be nothing more opposed to love and devotion than to despise and condemn your neighbor. Poking fun and scoffing are the same thing. Derision, mockery, scorn, and contempt are sins. There are some good-humored words that can be spoken in modest jesting that are acceptable. This is innocent fun. The Greeks called it *eutrapelia*. We call it pleasant conversation. With it we can have a friendly, amusing discussion about human imperfections.

The trick is to avoid moving from lighthearted mirth to vicious scoffing. Scoffing produces laughter through scorn and contempt of another. Laughing banter comes from freedom and familiarity in clever expression. Jokes and puns can be healthy. Saint Louis attended a dinner where a religious person wanted to discuss some difficult theological issues. The king spoke to all the guests. "This is not the moment for quoting texts. Let's enjoy each other by telling jokes and making puns!" He attempted to relax every one in his royal presence. The most devout also require a little time of recreation.

SNAP JUDGMENT

Our Savior says, "Do not judge, and you will not be judged. Do not condemn, and you will not be condemned. Forgive, and you will be forgiven" (Luke 6:37). The apostle Paul agrees. "Judge nothing before the appointed time; wait till the Lord comes. He will bring to light what is hidden in darkness and will expose the motives of men's hearts" (1 Corinthians 4:5). Hasty judgment is offensive to God. It is not our business to judge others. We are attempting to do God's business. God sees everything. We can only guess what is going on inside another person. We unfairly project our own motives. Another person's intention is "hidden in darkness." You would do better to judge yourself because you have plenty of data to work with. Make this a rule: Don't judge others; judge yourself. "If we judged ourselves, we would not come under judgment" (1 Corinthians 11:31). Too bad we aren't able to do it this way. It seems a natural thing to pass judgment frequently on our neighbor while ignoring our own imperfect selves. We do what is forbidden and ignore what is required.

Some people have a more difficult time controlling the urge to criticize others. Certain individuals are sour by nature. They are bitter and tend to be harsh with others. The prophet says of them, "You have turned justice into poison and the fruit of righteousness into bitterness" (Amos 6:12). People like this need to place themselves under the care of a competent spiritual director. Their bitterness is inbred and is extremely difficult to control or cure.

A curious twist to this is fairly commonplace. Sometimes we think that by putting another person down, we are building ourselves up. If we are looking down on others, it seems to follow that we must be somewhat higher. The foolish Pharisee in the temple prayed, "God, I thank you that I am not like other men—robbers, evildoers, adulterers—or even like this tax collector" (Luke 18:11).

Most of us are not prideful to such an extreme as the Pharisee. We simply notice the imperfections of others and feel a little satisfaction that the problems we observe are not things that hinder us. This process is extremely subtle. We rarely recognize it in ourselves even when someone points it out to us.

In a curious twist, we often accuse others of the very flaws we have ourselves. Somehow this has a way of mitigating our own sense of guilt. Others enjoy demonstrating their ability to analyze personality and character. They demonstrate their own intelligence by playfully probing the behavior of other people. There are also those who approve or condemn in conformity with their own taste. Love, in an unhealthy extreme, can degenerate into jealousy. If someone who is an object of love should smile a little at another person, it is taken as an indication of unfaithfulness or adultery. In the same way, our anxiety and ambition can make us suspicious of others and we judge them rashly.

Love never goes looking for evil. Love prefers to look away and hopes that it was not actually an evil but something that merely seemed to be. If it cannot be doubted, then love at least does not dwell on it.

Pliny describes *ophiusa,* an Egyptian herb that can induce hallucinations. Those who drink its juice imagine snakes and other frightening creatures surround them. When you drink the juices of conceit, jealousy, ambition, and loathing, you will consider everything around you to be foul. You will be quickly judgmental. Palm wine is an antidote for those who imbibe *ophiusa.* The cure for the rest of us is to drink as deeply as we can of the wine of genuine love. It will release you from the negative attitude that distorts your perception of reality. A jaundiced eye perceives the world tinted yellow. Hasty and ill-informed judgment is spiritual jaundice. When a person's eye has this affliction, everything looks evil. The cure is not a medication for the eye or even for the brain. It must be applied to the affections. If you have a kind heart, you will also make kind judgments.

There are some beautiful illustrations of this in the Bible. When traveling, Isaac identified Rebecca as his sister because he was afraid to admit she was his wife. "Abimelech king of the Philistines looked down from a

window and saw Isaac caressing his wife Rebekah. So Abimelech sum-
moned Isaac and said, 'She is really your wife! Why did you say, "She is my
sister?"'" (Genesis 26:8-9). He jumped to a correct conclusion immediately. If his eye was malicious, he would have concluded that she was a
harlot or that Isaac was guilty of incest. Abimelech came up with the most
wholesome conclusion based on the evidence he had witnessed.

It is our responsibility, Philothea, to produce the most charitable judgments we can regarding our neighbors. If their activities can be interpreted
from a variety of angles, pick the kindest one first.

When Mary became pregnant, Joseph quickly understood his fiancée
was a holy woman. He could not believe that this pure, angelic woman
could have been unfaithful to him. Rather than pass judgment on her, he
left the matter with God. If any man ever had good reason for reaching a
rash conclusion, it was Joseph. What constrained him? The New Testament gives us the answer. It tells us he was "a righteous man" (Matthew
1:19). A righteous person is sometimes faced with facts that cannot be
interpreted easily. There are too many unknowns, too many possibilities.
Instead of reaching a conclusion, the thing to do is to let God do the judging. Our Savior did as much for those who nailed him to the cross. He
gave them the benefit of the doubt, arguing they were ignorant. "Father,
forgive them, for they do not know what they are doing" (Luke 23:34).
An inexcusable sin can be opened to compassion by considering that it
may be the result of ignorance or weakness.

We never have any justification for passing judgment on others. Even
in court, God does the judging. The court officers are God's functionaries.
If they act out of their own emotion and notions, they are then passing
judgment and will be judged. There is nothing wrong with being suspicious and judging if clear evidence makes it necessary. If the activity
observed is open to multiple interpretations, it is then a wrong thing to
rush to judgment. I'll explain this more thoroughly in a later section.

If you have a sensitive conscience, you will not use snap judgment
regarding others. Bees remain in their hives on foggy days. We should

avoid probing into the partially known and cloudy activities of our neighbors. Instead, let's remain in our own hearts and make some strong resolutions to amend our own behavior. It is a waste of time for a soul to entertain itself with imagined things about other people.

The only exception to this are those who are responsible for management of others. For overseers, it is a necessary part of the job to watch, direct, and criticize those under them. Having done this, they then need to examine themselves honestly.

SLANDER

If you rob your neighbor of a good reputation, you have the obligation of making reparation. You can't enter heaven carrying someone else's property. Of all external possessions, a good name is most important. Slander is a form of murder.

With a single stroke of the tongue you can commit three murders. You kill your own soul, the soul of anyone who hears your slanderous comments, and the social life of your victim. It is spiritual homicide. Saint Bernard says that the slanderer has the devil on the tongue, and the one who listens to slander has the devil in the ear. A snake tongue is forked with two points. So also is the slanderer's tongue. It poisons the listener as well as the one being spoken against.

Beware of falsely accusing another person. It is not your business to expose someone's secret sins or to exaggerate the ones already made public. You are wrong to put an evil interpretation on a person's good works or to maliciously degrade those good works with your words.

People who preface slander with comments about doing "the right thing" or who make little private jokes are the most vicious slanderers of them all. "I really like him," they say. "In every other regard he is a fine man, but the truth must be told." "She was a nice girl, but she must have been caught at a weak moment." It is obvious what they are doing. When shooting an arrow, the archer pulls it back as near to himself as he can.

This gives more power to the shot. Those who appear to draw slander near themselves are merely making it penetrate the target audience more deeply. Slanderous joking is the most cruel of all. Hemlock is not a quick poison by itself. There is time to take an antidote. When hemlock is taken with wine, there is no antidote for it. In the same way slander that might pass lightly in one ear and out the other, sticks in the mind when it is told with a funny story.

Do not report that someone is a drunkard even if you have seen that person drunk. Refrain from saying that so-and-so is an adulterer even if that person has been caught in the act. A single experience is not enough to justify such a label. The sun stood still once to help Joshua win a battle, and it was darkened for our Savior's victory, yet we don't say that the sun is stationary or dark. Noah got drunk once. Lot got drunk twice. Neither man was a drunkard. Saint Peter blasphemed, but that did not make him blasphemous. To earn the title it must be habitual. It is not right to call someone quick-tempered or a thief on the basis of one observation.

Even if someone is addicted to vice for a long time, we risk falsehood if we label that person. Simon the leper called Mary Magdalene a sinner. She certainly had been a sinner not long before, but she was not any longer. She was sincerely penitent. Jesus took up for her. God's goodness is so vast that it can change character. How can we be certain that someone who was a sinner yesterday is the same today? Never draw conclusions based on yesterday.

We can easily make a serious mistake while trying to avoid slanderous comments about others. We can actually stumble into the trap of speaking of a fault in terms of praise. If you mention someone who has a sharp tongue, don't say he speaks unreservedly and with frankness. Someone who is vain need not be characterized as polite and refined. Rebelliousness does not need to be glorified as fervor. Insolence is not candor. While being careful not to speak ill of others, it is not necessary to say anything supportive of evil. It is necessary to call a spade a spade. If something is worthy of condemnation, let it be condemned. Bad things can be said about bad things. We only need to follow a few principles.

We may speak against someone's ideas or behavior only if it may help the one being spoken about or the ones who are listening. We must limit our comments to what is necessary without speaking one word too many. Never add any degree of heinousness to a crime. Make nothing sound worse than it is. I try to use my own tongue like a surgeon uses a scalpel. As the surgeon carefully cuts between nerves and tendons, I try to make a comment that neither exaggerates nor minimizes the truth. Here is the rule to follow: When you must condemn a vice, spare as far as possible the person in whom it is found.

We can speak openly of infamous, notorious public sinners if we are compassionate rather than arrogant. We should take no pleasure in the mistakes of others. It is our duty to denounce as sternly as possible schismatic sects and their leaders. It is an act of love to cry out against the wolf when it is among the sheep.

People are naturally critical of those who are in positions of power and responsibility. Politicians are naturally subject to criticism. We can even be disdainful of entire nations. This is not only offensive to the God of us all, but it can also get you into many arguments.

If you overhear negative comments about another person, do your best to make any allegation seem unlikely. If truth will not allow that, then attempt to discover some mitigating circumstance. Failing in these things, show sympathy for the accused and bring up another subject. Let everyone present with you understand that if you have escaped that particular sin, it is because of God's grace. Gently remind the one gossiping of his or her personal imperfections. If you can think of any, give an account of some kindness done by the one being criticized.

In all your conversation, use clear, unequivocal, honest language. If you have nothing to hide, there is no need to speak ambiguously. It may not be a good thing for you to report everything you know. At the same time, let everything you report be true. God is "the God of truth" (Psalm 31:5). If you inadvertently give out some misinformation, correct it immediately.

Manipulative, tricky statements are an attempt to obscure the truth. Holy Scripture assures us that God is not associated with "cunning stratagem" (Wisdom 1:5, *Anchor Bible*). Simple, honest business is always best. The art of making deals belongs to this world's children. God's children walk the straight and narrow without guile. "You will be safe, if you always do right, but you will get caught, if you are dishonest" (Proverbs 10:9, CEV). Falsifying, misrepresentation, and deception are not a part of the devout life. David sang, "I will watch my ways and keep my tongue from sin; I will put a muzzle on my mouth" (Psalm 39:1). "Set a guard over my mouth, O LORD; keep watch over the door of my lips" (Psalm 141:3).

Saint Louis urged us to stay out of arguments and bickering. He thought it best if we never contradicted anyone unless it was extremely hazardous to let the comment pass. If it becomes necessary to correct someone's idea, then use care and delicacy. There is no need to provoke anger. Rudeness will get you nowhere. Ancient wisdom advises us to speak few words and to speak none that are purposeless. The quality of our comments is as important as the quantity. My advice is moderation. If you are too reserved and do not join in conversations, others may misinterpret your behavior as timidity or contempt. If you are constantly running your mouth rather than listening to others, they will conclude that you are a superficial and frivolous person.

RECREATION AND SPORTS

It is important to take a break now and then. Recreation relaxes both mind and body. Cassian tells us that a hunter found Saint John cradling a living bird in his hand and gently petting its neck. The hunter asked him why he was wasting his time like that. John asked him why he didn't keep his bow always taut. "It would lose its spring if I did," the hunter answered. The apostle replied, "Then don't be surprised if I relax sometimes. After a little recreation I can concentrate better."

It is a mistake to be so strict, driven, and abstemious that you can neither play a little yourself nor allow others a little diversion. Get out into the open air. Have some fun! Play the lute, sing, go hunting. Enjoy some innocent recreation. The only requirement is enough discretion to give it a proper time, place, and quantity.

Many sports are worthwhile. Tennis, pall-mall, charging the ring, chess, and backgammon are examples of games that increase physical ability and stimulate mental activity. These are excellent recreation. Limit the amount of time you give them and keep the stakes small. If you push yourself too hard, you will end up exhausting your body and mind rather than refreshing them. If the stakes are too high, your emotions will be uncontrollable. Anyway, it is not good to wager a lot of money on such trifling activities. On games of chance, where skill and effort are not involved, it makes no sense at all.

The point, Philothea, is not to become obsessed with any amusement. Even if your favorite recreation is a good and healthy one, it is not good to become overly distracted and consumed by it. Go ahead and enjoy your games, but don't let them keep you from other more important things.

Games of chance, such as dice and cards, are risky recreations. You may wonder what harm there could be in them. Gain should come as the result of labor and not as a random reward. The only pleasure in gambling is winning, and that pleasure results from another's loss and pain. This is certainly evil.

Balls and dances are recreations that are morally neutral, but the manner in which they are conducted can push them toward hazardous evil. Because these night parties are held in nearly dark conditions, there is a natural invitation to unseemly behavior. Staying up late at night robs the dancers of the morning after. It is never a good idea to substitute night for day, darkness for light, depraved behavior for works of love. A dance is a setting for some very poor choices.

If you want my opinion, Philothea, I feel about dances the way a doctor considers pumpkins and mushrooms. The best of them are worthless. If you insist upon eating pumpkins, make sure they are properly cooked. If you are obligated to be present at a dance, monitor your own behavior. Display decency, self-respect, and the best intentions. Doctors advise us to eat mushrooms only occasionally. Regardless of the care given to their preparation, too many of them will make us sick. Let your attendance at dances also be infrequent. Doctors tell us that a glass of good wine is the best chaser for mushrooms. When the dance is over, contemplate good and holy things.

Card playing and dancing can be kept from getting out of control by seeing to it that they remain recreation. Don't let them dominate your life. Stop before you are exhausted. Never permit fun to turn into work. Make sure that your participation is a natural expression of friendliness.

INCONVENIENCES

"You have stolen my heart with one glance of your eyes, with one jewel of your necklace" (Song of Songs 4:9). Eyes are of tremendous value, but beads are trifles. The holy Bridegroom shows a willingness to accept both the great and the small, the major and the minor. He wants us to serve him in grand and sacrificial ways but also in ordinary and seemingly insignificant ways. Our devotion at either extreme will attract him.

Philothea, always be prepared to offer great sacrifices and to suffer dreadful afflictions for our Lord if that is what he wants. These are on a level with the value of your eyes. Be ready to give what is asked of you. Ordinarily, God will not make such demands. On these ordinary days you can give him an important sacrifice of small things, a jewel from your necklace. Patiently endure life's little insults and injuries. Accept inconveniences and little setbacks. These little trifles add up. They become attractive to our Lord. Acts of charity, toothaches, headaches, bad colds, a temperamental family member, broken dishes, a nasty remark, a lost ring or handkerchief can be accepted with love. This is pleasing to God. "And if anyone gives even a cup of cold water to one of these little ones because he is my disciple, I tell you the truth, he will certainly not lose his reward" (Matthew 10:42). Such opportunities will come your way steadily. Employ them well and you will accumulate enormous spiritual treasure.

The depth of spirituality impressed me when I read the life of Saint Catherine of Siena. She was often enraptured and spoke profoundly on religious subjects. I am sure that the contemplative glance of her eye stole the heart of her heavenly Bridegroom. At the same time, I am struck by the way she performed humble daily tasks for the love of God. Her work in the kitchen and household was warmed and made a joy by her devotion. Her little meditations while kindling fires and dressing meat are as impressive to me as her more spectacular ecstasies and visions.

Saint Catherine developed a technique any one of us could emulate. While cooking food she thought of herself as Martha in her kitchen at Bethany preparing a meal for our Savior. In this way we can direct every menial task to God as divine service.

It is a rare moment that gives us an opportunity to do something truly grand for God. Small opportunities come regularly and frequently. Our Savior will say, "Well done, good and faithful servant! You have been faithful with a few things; I will put you in charge of many things. Come and share your master's happiness!" (Matthew 25:21). "So whether you eat or drink or whatever you do, do it all for the glory of God" (1 Corinthians 10:31). Your sleeping and daily chores will take on new meaning and become an avenue of God's blessing.

BEING REASONABLE

The distinguishing mark of being human is rationality. How strange that we rarely encounter a reasonable person. Examples of commonplace irrationality are easy to find. We are critical of our neighbor for little faults while overlooking greater faults of our own. We want to buy cheap and sell high. We want justice for others and mercy for ourselves. We think our ideas are worth attention but place little value on the ideas of others. We are controlled by our own taste and denigrate the taste of others. We prefer to be around good-looking and well-dressed people. We favor the rich over the poor. We make a big fuss over some act of charity we perform and complain that we, in turn, are neglected. We use two different scales. With one that is rigged in our favor we weigh our own behavior. With the other we weigh our neighbors' behavior and find it lacking. "Do not have two differing weights in your bag—one heavy, one light. Do not have two differing measures in your house—one large, one small. You must have accurate and honest weights and measures" (Deuteronomy 25:13-15).

Try to put yourself in the other person's position. Think of yourself as the seller when you buy and as the buyer when you sell. You will lose nothing because you are reasonably generous. A clear indicator of reason is your ability to "do to others what you would have them do to you" (Matthew 7:12).

It is unreasonable to focus desire on distant or impractical things. When I am seriously ill there is little point in wishing I could visit other sick people, preach, or do heavy labor. These would be more than I could possibly do. Worrying about such things takes energy that could be given to the more immediate opportunities of practicing patience, acceptance, and humility. Sometimes we are called upon to stay in bed and suffer. That is our spiritual assignment for the moment. We are often like the pregnant woman who desires fruit that is out of season— cherries in autumn and grapes in spring. Instead of wishing you had the ability to serve God in other ways, serve God with the abilities you already have.

There is nothing wrong with making long-range plans, of dreaming about the possibilities of the future. The important thing is to start where you are right now. Put distant desires into some corner of your being and wait for the proper time to arrive. Pick fruit that is in season. This is good advice for both the pious and the secular. Living any other way is to worry and be distracted.

FAMILY LIFE

"Marriage should be honored by all" (Hebrews 13:4). If only God's beloved Son could be invited to attend every wedding as he was to the marriage at Cana. It is more commonplace to invite Adonis or Venus instead of our Lord and our Lady. A healthy marriage begins with reflection upon the divine significance of the union.

Little is to be gained by exhorting married couples to love one another with *natural* love. Neither is it helpful to urge them to love each other with *human* love. Listen to the apostle, "Husbands, love your wives, just as Christ loved the church and gave himself up for her" (Ephesians 5:25). I will add: Wives, love your husbands as the church loves Christ. God brought you together. Divine love is yours to share.

The results of recognizing a divine dimension to your marriage are remarkable. First of all, it will last. It is an adhesive that will bond you together. Two sticks of wood that have been properly glued together are easier to break in some other place than the joint. Second, there will be a sacred fidelity of each partner in the union. A total commitment to the marriage will be expressed in constant faithfulness to each other. Ultimately, you cooperate with God in the rearing of children. You recognize the fact that God places a living soul in your care.

The most beautiful apple in the barrel may harbor a worm. An exemplary marriage may be ruined by jealousy. Jealousy is love that has gone bad. It causes rot. There will be arguments, bitterness, and divorce. While jealousy might display to some degree the size of a friendship, it has nothing to say about the purity and superiority of it. Expect of your partner no more than you give. Do you want a faithful spouse? Then be faithful. "It is God's will that you should be sanctified: that you should avoid sexual immorality; that each of you should learn to control his own body in a way that is holy and honorable, not in passionate lust like the heathen, who do not know God" (1 Thessalonians 4:3-5).

God-inspired love can create a mutual support so strong that both partners will never be angry with each other at the same moment. Major arguments and disputes simply will not happen. Honeybees will not remain long in noisy places. Neither is the Holy Spirit comfortable in homes where there is yelling, discord, bickering, and bitter strife.

Temptations and Setbacks

O nce it becomes evident that you intend to live a devout life, secular people will laugh at you and criticize you. The worst of them will say that because of some hard experiences you have run to God as an escape. Your friends will warn you of the unhappy consequences of your choice, saying that you will lose your reputation, become difficult to work with, or age prematurely. They will tell you that if you are going to live in the world, you must be a part of the world. They will call you an extremist and urge moderation upon you.

These foolish babblers are not concerned about you, Philothea. "If you belonged to the world, it would love you as its own. As it is, you do not belong to the world, but I have chosen you out of the world. That is why the world hates you" (John 15:19).

Let some throw away many nights playing chess or cards, and no one says anything about it. But if we give an hour to meditation, they are ready to go for the doctor to cure us of our illness. The world is a biased judge, approving its own and dealing harshly with the children of God.

The only way to please the world is to become totally immersed in it. It has an insatiable appetite for you. Its demands are unending. If it is known that we are Christian and that we go along with the world and play its games, it will be horrified. If we refuse to dance to its tune, it will then call us hypocrites. If we dress well, people of the world will think we have some personal agenda. If we wear rags, they will say we are cheap and parsimonious. If we laugh, it will think us frivolous. If we weep, we are sullen. We will never please the world. It will magnify our imperfections. If the world cannot fault our actions, it will condemn our motives. The wolf is not selective. It will eat black and white sheep, with or without horns. Regardless of our activity, the world will declare war upon us. It is not worth worrying about. Stick with the devout life. Comets are as bright in the night as planets. The planets endure, but comets fade. In the same way, hypocrisy can appear to be honest virtue. In time, hypocrisy dissolves in a puff of smoke while virtue remains steady. "The world has been crucified to me, and I to the world" (Galatians 6:14). If the world considers us foolish, let us consider the world insane.

While light is a good thing, it can blind us after we have been in the dark. The change in your style of life, Philothea, may create some problems. Everything is so unfamiliar. Be patient. This strangeness will eventually wear off. The challenge that the climbing of such a high mountain as the practice of Christianity places in front of you can be daunting. You will consider it to be impossible. Take courage! Young bees are called nymphs. They are not able to fly and collect honey from flowers. Gradually, after feasting on the honey prepared by older bees, they begin to develop. Eventually, they also fly and work like the others. Accept the fact that you are now a nymph in the devout life. In due time, you will develop wings of your own. To help you through some of the rough places, I will prepare you to deal with temptation, anxiety, and sadness.

TEMPTATION

Temptation works in a simple way. First, the soul perceives a suggestion to sin. Next, the soul responds either positively or negatively, finding the suggestion appealing or disgusting. Then it decides yes or no. These three simple steps lead in opposite directions, depending upon the soul's response. It may be temptation, pleasure, and agreement. Or it may be temptation, displeasure, and refusal.

We may be tempted by a certain sin all our lives, but if we refuse to yield, God is not displeased with us. We are passive recipients of temptation. If we are not pleased by what is happening to us, there is no need to feel guilty for having been tempted. Be strong when you are tempted, Philothea.

You have not been defeated as long as the experience is unpleasant for you. There is a vast difference between being tempted and yielding to it.

The soul is not uniform. There are higher and lower areas. The inferior part of the soul does not consistently agree with the superior part. It may act independently. It may enjoy being tempted even though it does not give in. This struggle is the tension reported by the apostle when he wrote, "For the sinful nature desires what is contrary to the Spirit, and the Spirit what is contrary to the sinful nature" (Galatians 5:17). Paul described the warfare in his soul: "When I want to do good, evil is right there with me. For in my inner being I delight in God's law; but I see another law at work in the members of my body, waging war against the law of my mind and making me a prisoner of the law of sin at work within my members" (Romans 7:21-23).

Perhaps you have seen a fireplace where a large fire burned the night before. In the morning it is nothing but a heap of gray ashes. If someone begins to search for some fire, it may be possible to find a little at the very center of the ashes if they are carefully raked. It will be enough to start another fire. Love works the same way in our spiritual life. The pleasure of temptation pushes the love of God deep into the soul. It hides it in a small space under spiritual ashes. It is not evident anywhere else and is barely perceptible in the innermost area of the soul. But it is actually there. The pleasure of the poorer area of the soul brings displeasure to the better area. It may envelop and cover the will, but it does not invade it. Any pleasure is unintentional and therefore is not sinful.

An impressive example of this can be found in the life of Saint Catherine of Siena. She struggled with sexual temptations for a considerable period of time. Afterward, she asked the Lord where he had been when she was nearly overwhelmed by such thoughts. He replied that he was in her heart. She asked him how that could be possible. Could he live in such a polluted place as her heart had been? Our Lord asked her if her thoughts had brought her pleasure or pain. She replied that they had brought her grief.

He assured her that if he had not been present, she would have been over-come and defeated. He had given her the ability to resist the temptations. Her personal struggle had actually increased her strength.

A doctor knows how to feel the heart of someone who appears to be dead. If he perceives the slightest motion, he understands there is a good chance to help that person recover. Sometimes it may seem that we are absolutely overcome by temptation. Spiritual life has virtually succumbed. Then place your hand on your soul's heart. See if there is any sign of life. It may well be that you will discover our Lord Jesus Christ, though hidden and covered with ashes, is still living in your soul. With the application of prayer, sacraments, and trust in God, you will recover and live a good life.

Sometimes we invite disaster. If I know in advance that certain places will tempt me and I go there anyway, I am guilty of each temptation that comes my way. It is also reprehensible for someone to go looking for improper advances while entertaining no thought at all of agreeing to par-ticipate in an affair.

When you are tempted, immediately do what children do when they are in the woods and see a wolf or a bear. They run into the arms of their parents. At the very least they cry out to them for assistance and safety. Run to God in a similar manner. Ask for his help. Our Lord tells us to do this. "Watch and pray so that you will not fall into temptation. The spirit is willing, but the body is weak" (Matthew 26:41).

If the temptation persists or becomes even more appealing, spiritually approach the cross upon which Christ is crucified. Throw your arms around it. Affirm that you will not yield to the temptation and implore him to give you strength to resist it. The way to deal with temptations is to look away from them and at the Lord. If you pay any attention to the temptation itself, it will weaken your resolve.

The very best cure for temptations is to discuss them frankly with your spiritual director. Keeping a temptation secret is the first step to destruction. If you are still subject to temptations, continue to resist. There is no sin as long as you say no. Use the response of our Savior. "Away from me, Satan! For it is written: 'Worship the Lord your God, and serve him only'" (Matthew 4:10). When a devout soul is tempted, there is no time for debate or discussion. Simply turn to Jesus Christ and restate your love and continuing devotion.

For every great temptation there will be many small ones. Wolves and bears are more dangerous than flies, but the latter bothers us most. You many never murder anyone, but you will certainly become angry. You may avoid adultery, but it is not easy to control your eyes. You may never steal anything from your neighbor, but you may covet it.

Let these flies and gnats buzz around you. Instead of fighting with them, do the very opposite of what the temptation is suggesting. For instance, if you are tempted to be vain, think about the troubles of others. If you are greedy, remember how death will take it all away from you and then go give something away or pass up a profit. Make the effort and you will be hardened against future temptations.

ANXIETY

After sin, anxiety is the worst thing that can afflict a soul. It is the result of a strong desire to escape a present evil or to reach a desired goal. But anxiety increases the pain and prevents the attainment. Birds that are caught in nets flap and flutter wildly in an effort to escape, but they only become more thoroughly trapped. When you want to get out of a bad situation and go to a good one, be sure you are calm and deliberate. I am not recommending carelessness, but an unhurried, untroubled approach to solving your problems. Without this, you may make a mess of things and have even more difficulty.

At the first sign of anxiety, pray to God. Talk with your spiritual director or some other friend. Sharing your grief unburdens your soul. It is the best remedy for anxiety.

SADNESS

"Godly sorrow brings repentance that leads to salvation and leaves no regret, but worldly sorrow brings death" (2 Corinthians 7:10). Sadness, then, is both a blessing and a curse. It has many negative but only two positive effects—compassion for others and repentance.

The negative responses include worry, indolence, rage, distrust, jealousy, and impatience. Observing this, a wise person said, "Worry never did anybody any good, and it has destroyed many people. It will make you old before your time. Jealousy and anger will shorten your life" (Sirach 30:23-24, TEV).

Misdirected sorrow is like a killing winter. It harms the soul by increasing fear and making prayer distasteful. It can dull our ability to think clearly. It robs us of our strength. Our spiritual life is incapacitated.

"Is any one of you in trouble? He should pray" (James 5:13). It is also helpful to get busy with some diverting work. Get around spiritual people and talk out your feelings with them. Keep trusting God. After this trial he will deliver you from evil.

Each day is unique. There are cloudy days and sunny, wet days and dry, windy days and calm. The seasons roll by as day turns into night and night into day. This variety produces beauty. And so it is with your life. There are ups and downs. No two days, no two hours, are ever exactly alike.

The challenge for us is to remain stable and steady even as everything around us is changing. Our path is set toward God. A compass needle always points north regardless of the ship's course. No wind will shake it from its homing on the North Star. If we will aspire toward God, the confusing changes of life will not unsteady us.

Our soul is capable of being overcome with sadness or gladness, with kindness or acrimony, with peace or difficulty, with light or darkness, with provocation or tranquility, with delight or disgust, with emptiness or compassion. It may be charred by the sun or revived by the dew. Amid all this upheaval, the compass needle of our spirit will never fail to lead us toward the love of God, its Creator, Savior, and only good. "If we live, we live to the Lord; and if we die, we die to the Lord. So, whether we live or die, we belong to the Lord" (Romans 14:8). "Who shall separate us from the love of Christ? Shall trouble or hardship or persecution or famine or nakedness or danger or sword?... Neither death nor life, neither angels nor demons, neither the present nor the future, nor any powers, neither height nor depth, nor anything else in all creation, will be able to separate us from the love of God that is in Christ Jesus our Lord" (Romans 8:35,38-39).

Our determination to always seek the merciful love of God balances our life. It gives us a sacred stability amid all the changes and surprises that come our way. When little bees are caught in a storm, they take hold of small stones so that they can keep their balance when they fly. Our firm resolution to stay with God is like ballast to the soul amid the rolling waves of life.

FALSE DEVOTION

Devotion is often misrepresented. Actually, true devotion does not result in many of the expectations of popular thought. It is not a matter of being moved to tears. Spiritual exercises are not intended to bring us some sort of delicious experience. Philothea, it is possible to be touched with powerful religious emotion and still be a malicious person. Clearly, such individuals demonstrate that they have neither a vital love of God nor an authentic devotion. When Saul chased David into the wilderness, he entered a cave where David and his men were hiding. David had opportunities to kill Saul, but he spared his life. As Saul was leaving in safety, David called out to Saul to prove his own innocence and to demonstrate his mercy. Saul was touched. He called David his child, wept, and thanked him. There could have been no greater display of sweetness and tenderness on Saul's part. Even so, Saul's heart had not changed, and he did not cease from pursuing David with cruelty.

In the same way, some people think about God's goodness and our Savior's passion and feel a great tenderness of heart. They may even utter sighs and tearful prayers. They seem to be filled with intense devotion. But when a test comes, what a difference! A passing shower in the hot summer sends down great drops of rain. They fall to earth but do not sink in. All they produce is mushrooms. Likewise, these tender tears fail to penetrate the heart. For all the display of devotion, they will not contribute a penny of their ill-gotten wealth. They will not surrender one of their perversities. They will not endure the least inconvenience for the service of the suffering Christ they were just weeping over. Any good feelings they get from their moment of devotion are nothing but spiritual mushrooms.

These things play tricks on us. They keep us from looking for a more authentic devotion to God. True devotion is a constant, determined, prompt, and active will to do what we know pleases God.

We are like the child who cries when he sees the doctor draw blood from his mother, and yet he disobeys his mother when she asks for the apple or candy he is holding in his hand. He refuses to give it to her. In our devotions, we are moved to tears when we meditate on the wound opened in Christ's side during his crucifixion. Such a sorrowful moment is worthy of our tears. But then we refuse to give him some "apple" we clutch for ourselves. We do not surrender our heart. We cling to petty distractions and gratifications because they are our "candy," and we prefer them to God's grace. We are like children—emotional yet frail, willful, and ineffectual. Religious excitement has little to do with true devotion and may actually mislead us.

All of which is not to say that there are never any pleasant results from acts of devotion. It was such religious experience that prompted David to sing, "How sweet are your words to my taste, sweeter than honey to my mouth!" (Psalm 119:103). After you have had such a moment, everything else takes second place. The world has nothing to offer that is superior or equal. Such experiences are little appetizers, a hint of what is in store for the soul that truly loves God. They are treats that God hands out to his children, cordials of reward. Pliny reports that Alexander the Great was led to Arabia by the aromas that drifted out to his ship at sea. The odors of earth picked up the spirits of his entire crew. As we travel the sea of this life, we can catch a little sniff of what is waiting for us in heaven.

Some of the perceptions that result from a life of devotion are helpful and others can be harmful. How can you tell the difference? "By their fruit you will recognize them. Do people pick grapes from thornbushes, or figs from thistles?" (Matthew 7:16). Think of your heart as a tree. The branches are your emotions. The fruits are your activity and accomplishments. If the pleasures of devotion make you more unassuming, persevering, flexible, loving, and caring of your neighbor, more faithful and cooperative and sincere, then, Philothea, you can be sure they are gifts from God. If they please only you and make you egotistic, brusque, argumentative, impatient, stubborn, arrogant, brash, and critical of your neighbor while you think you are a little saint who does not need direction or correction, then without doubt, they are not from God. A good tree bears good fruit.

Never take any pride in the pleasant results of meditation. They do not mean you are a good person, and they have little power to make you better. They are gifts from God. You can live a devout life without them. "The Lord is good to those whose hope is in him" (Lamentations 3:25). If you have sugar in your mouth you cannot claim that your mouth is sweet. It is the sugar that is sweet. Spiritual gifts may be sweet. Undoubtedly, the God who gives them is supremely good. There is no indication the one chosen to receive such gifts is good. Instead, we are like children who need a little treat, something to draw us nearer to loving God. If there is anything outstanding about the little courtesies and gifts that may bless our devotional life, it is the fact that God gives them to us. Think of God as being like a mother who occasionally puts a little candy in her child's mouth to bring him pleasure. As the child grows up, he begins to prefer his mother's hugs and nearness.

Why does God sometimes grant us a moment of spiritual joy? They are intended to make us better neighbors and to love God even more. As a mother gives a child a piece of candy in order to receive a kiss, let's respond to our Savior with a kiss. We kiss him by obeying his command and doing what he wants us to do. If we ever receive any kind of spiritual blessing, let's immediately set about doing good for others and becoming more humble.

Most important, don't begin your spiritual exercises with any high expectation of divine favors. We are to seek God, not God's gifts. We must be prepared to continue in the devout life even if we never receive any kind of spiritual apéritif. Whether we are on Calvary or the Mount of Transfiguration, let's say with Peter, "Lord, it is good for us to be here" (Matthew 17:4). If God grants you a special favor in your spiritual life, discuss it calmly with your spiritual director. You may need help to control yourself in this regard. "If you find honey, eat just enough—too much of it, and you will vomit" (Proverbs 25:16).

DRY TIMES

Weather changes. There are times when rains are plentiful and times of drought. You will experience seasons of spiritual dryness. Your soul will not seem to have the slightest interest in prayer and the spiritual life. You will feel like you are lost in a trackless desert. You will not see a single path that leads to God. There will be no water that will quench your thirst. You will understand David when he lamented, "As the deer pants for streams of water, so my soul pants for you, O God. My soul thirsts for God, for the living God. When can I go and meet with God? My tears have been my food day and night, while men say to me all day long, 'Where is your God?'" (Psalm 42:1-3).

The thing to do at such times, Philothea, is to seek the origin of the dryness. Often, we bring it upon ourselves. If a child is sick, her mother may withhold sweet treats. God also recognizes certain conditions in us when it would not be good to provide us with spiritual comfort. "It was good for me to be afflicted so that I might learn your decrees" (Psalm 119:71). "Before I was afflicted I went astray" (Psalm 119:67).

We may also miss an opportunity with God. The Israelites had only one chance each day to harvest God's manna in the desert. "Each morning everyone gathered as much as he needed, and when the sun grew hot, it melted away" (Exodus 16:21).

Sometimes we get distracted. Christ knocks at our door, but we are too preoccupied to answer. He does not force his way in on us. He leaves us to our amusements. Then, when we decide to look for him again, he may not be easy to find. As I say, we bring this upon ourselves. Hang on to Egypt's flour and you will not receive heaven's manna. Bees are repelled by artificial scents. The Holy Spirit is not comfortable around the false earthly pleasures. Jesus' mother, Mary, said, "He has filled the hungry with good things but has sent the rich away empty" (Luke 1:53).

Even our conversations with our spiritual director may result in spiritual aridity. This is because we play insincere little spiritual games. We pretend to be something other than we really are. Our comments are misleading. If we are not as guileless as a child, we should not expect to receive a child's treats.

There is one other consideration. Do you cling to the results of what you have been given? If you do, you will be given more. "For everyone who has will be given more, and he will have an abundance. Whoever does not have, even what he has will be taken from him" (Matthew 25:29). A plant in leaf is blessed by rainfall. A dormant plant may rot when wet.

It is because of things like these that we sometimes experience spiritual dryness. Check it out, Philothea. Don't worry about it. If you discover a reason of your own making, thank God for the revelation. Spiritual sickness begins to be cured once we find out its cause.

Now what if you simply can't explain your aridity of soul? Perhaps no clear reason emerges. There are some things you need to do.

Begin by admitting your personal inadequacy. "Dear Lord, by myself

I am nothing but dry soil waiting for a shower of rain. I am dust, blowing in the wind."

Then ask for God's help. "My Father, if it is possible, may this cup be taken from me" (Matthew 26:39). "Awake, north wind, and come, south wind! Blow on my garden, that its fragrance may spread abroad" (Song of Songs 4:16).

Have a frank discussion with someone you trust. Be alert for good guidance. Sometimes the most innocuous advice turns out to be wonderfully helpful. In the Old Testament there is a story of Naaman, a great warrior who had leprosy. The prophet Elisha told him that if he bathed in the Jordan River seven times he would be cured. "But Naaman went away angry and said, 'I thought that he would surely come out to me and stand and call on the name of the LORD his God, wave his hand over the spot and cure me of my leprosy. Are not...the rivers of Damascus, better than any of the waters of Israel? Couldn't I wash in them and be cleansed?' So he turned and went off in a rage" (2 Kings 5:11-12). It simply didn't make any sense. As it turned out, God used the Jordan River to heal Naaman.

After all of the efforts described above, the best thing to do is to simply accept spiritual dryness as a fact of life. Don't fret too much about getting out of it. Surrender to God. Serve him in the desert. Now is the time to add the remainder of Christ's prayer in the Garden of Gethsemane. "My Father, if it is possible, may this cup be taken from me. Yet not as I will, but as you will" (Matthew 26:39). Accept it calmly. God will be pleased to see such holy apathy. It was enough for God to see that Abraham was willing to sacrifice his son, Isaac. Job expressed it beautifully for us all: "The LORD gave and the LORD has taken away; may the name of the LORD be praised" (Job 1:21).

Be courageous. Wait patiently. Continue serving God and neighbor. Keep on with your devotional exercises. If we can't offer God moist, fresh fruit, then let us offer dried fruit. It makes no difference to God as long as our offering is an expression of love. When there are many flowers in an exceptional spring, the bees become so busy producing honey they neglect reproducing themselves. The same thing happens with a soul that is enjoying a gorgeous spiritual springtime. It enjoys God's gifts so much it becomes self-centered and neglects to do good works. On the other hand, spiritual dryness at times when there is no pleasant return for our devotion tends to increase such virtues as endurance, humility, and submission.

Let me make one additional comment. It is possible for this aridity of soul to be the result of overdoing our spiritual exercises. We fatigue ourselves with too much fasting, praying, and service. Our bodies get tired and our minds quickly follow. The only cure is rest and recreation. Saint Francis of Assisi pointed out that excessive work can dampen spiritual enthusiasm.

Renewing the Spiritual Life

If birds stop beating their wings, they quickly fall to the ground. Unless your soul works at holding itself up, your flesh will drag it down. Therefore, you must renew your determination regularly. Oddly, a spiritual crash leaves us lower than when we began. Clocks need regular winding, cleaning, and oiling. Sometimes they need repair. Similarly, we must care for our spiritual life by examining and servicing our hearts at least annually. Early Christians ordinarily took a spiritual inventory and renewed their vows on the date of our Lord's baptism. It would be good if we did the same.

Bring this up with your spiritual director. Agree on a proper time to take a spiritual retreat. Get alone, if you can. Meditate on two or three of the ideas below in the manner I described in part 2.

THE FIRST STEP

You are through with sin. It no longer attracts you. Your whole being has been dedicated to God. If you should stumble into sin, God will help you get up and put you on a better path. What could be better for you?

You have reached this agreement with none other than God. If we are bound by a legal contract with other people, think of the obligations we have to God. "My heart says of you, 'Seek his face!' Your face, LORD, I will seek" (Psalm 27:8). "My heart is stirred by a noble theme" (Psalm 45:1).

Remember that your promises to God were made in the presence of heavenly beings. Angels rejoiced. This joy in heaven will be repeated if you sincerely renew your vows.

And don't forget how this all came about. God was good to you. Is it not true that you were prompted to that moment by an action of the Holy Spirit? The cords that drew you toward this decision were woven of love.

God mercifully provided you with the sacraments, good reading, and prayer. You were sleeping, and God was taking care of you. "'For I know the plans I have for you,' declares the LORD, 'plans to prosper you and not to harm you, plans to give you hope and a future'" (Jeremiah 29:11). God lovingly meditated for you.

When was it that you were divinely inspired to take this action? Perhaps you were young. It is a blessing to take this step early. Saint Augustine regretted that he learned these lessons so late in life. Perhaps you can say with David, "Since my youth, O God, you have taught me, and to this day I declare your marvelous deeds" (Psalm 71:17). On the other hand, this may have come to you in your maturity. You have therefore received a tremendous gift. If you have thrown away your early years and then respond to God's love before your death, you can rejoice that the unhappy part of your experience is over. If this moment had not intervened, your distress would have continued through eternity.

What are the results? You are a different person now. Your life has improved. You are able now to really pray. It is like a conversation with God. You honestly love God. Whatever stood between you and God is gone. You have the privilege of greater familiarity with the church and sacraments. Try to measure the gifts of God! God is behind all of these things. "I will not die but live, and will proclaim what the LORD has done" (Psalm 118:17).

When you have reflected upon these things, offer a prayer of thanks. Ask the Lord to help you capitalize upon your gains. Emerge from this exercise with humble trust in God's love. It is still too soon to determine to deepen this relationship. Go on to the next step.

THE SECOND STEP

This part involves several different activities. It is not necessary to do everything at one time. Spread it out. Give one session to thinking about your responsibilities to God. Another day, ponder your relationship with others. Then find time to consider your emotional state. While it may be a good idea to begin and end each session on your knees, it is not helpful to remain in this posture the entire time. Take a walk or rest in bed (if you can stay awake). Before you can do this, you must carefully study what follows. It is important that you complete this entire process in no more than three days and two nights. Give it as much attention as you can each day. It will not be effective if you scatter the exercises over a longer span of time. Keep notes on your struggles and shortcomings. Such a list will remind you of topics to discuss with your spiritual director.

There is no need to completely isolate yourself from others while you do these things. It may be helpful to go to bed a little earlier than usual. You need to rest your mind and body.

Here is what to do.

Place yourself in God's presence.

Ask the Holy Spirit to inspire you, helping you to see yourself honestly. Pray Saint Augustine's humble prayer: "Lord, help me to know you and to know myself." Ask as Saint Francis of Assisi did, "Who are you, Lord, and who am I?" Insist that you have no prideful interest in reviewing your progress. The glory you seek is not your own but God's. Your object is to thank God for any advance you have made.

Insist that if you discover, as you expect, that you have not come very far, or perhaps have remained unchanged or even retrograded, then you will not be discouraged or depressed. Determine that such knowledge will only make you try harder, that you will fervently seek divine assistance.

Once you have done these things, quietly and humbly recall how you have lived prior to this moment. How have you related with God, your neighbor, and yourself?

SPIRITUAL INTROSPECTION

Is deadly sin a part of your life? Have you determined that you will never commit such an act? Have you kept your resolution? This is of primary importance. This is the base on which your spiritual life will develop.

Are you keeping God's commandments? Do they seem positive rather than negative to you? Do you welcome them as you would good food?

What about the little temptations? It is impossible to live well enough to escape them. They catch everyone. Ask yourself some important questions. Are there one or two that strongly attract you? Is there one that is a particular weakness for you?

Do you enjoy spiritual exercises? Do my suggestions make you uncomfortable? Are they repulsive? Which is your favorite? Would you rather hear the Bible read or read it yourself? Do you prefer to talk about the Scripture? Is meditation at the top of your list? Is confession or Communion or spiritual guidance your first choice? Are any of these activities undesirable for you? If you discover something that is less than appealing, try to determine why.

Do you enjoy being aware that you are in God's presence? Are thoughts about God pleasant for you? Do you naturally love God? Do thoughts of God's love produce a mellow feeling in you? Do you enjoy thinking about the greatness and goodness of God? Has your ordinary, daily business ever been interrupted by thoughts of God? Do you welcome such moments? Do you find yourself actually running out to meet God, as it were? For some people it is similar to the way a woman responds when her husband returns home from a long trip. The instant she hears him speak, even if she happens to be busily preoccupied with demanding responsibilities, she forgets everything else and thinks of the one who has come home. For the soul that loves God, nothing can distract attention. There is the overwhelming joy of a returning pleasant experience. This indicates an excellent spiritual condition.

Do you enjoy Jesus Christ? Honeybees delight in their honey while wasps prefer rotting things. In the same way, a devout soul is pleased to think about Jesus Christ and is naturally affectionate toward him. Others chase after vanities.

Do religious images appeal to you? Do stories of the saints inspire you? Do you love and trust those who watch from heaven? Do you speak openly and sincerely about God? Is it a pleasure to sing God's praise?

Have you made any sacrifice? Is there something you have denied yourself for God's sake? Love inspires giving. What have you surrendered for the love of God?

Do you love yourself? How would you characterize this love? Would you say it is a worldly love? In that case, you will spend all of your energy establishing a place for yourself here and have little regard for anything beyond this world. If your love is a heavenly love, you will at least want to be prepared to travel when it pleases the Lord to end your time here. A healthy love will cause us to love our soul more than our body. We will have a higher regard for the opinion of angels than the opinion of others.

You will not think much of yourself in God's presence. A fly is not much when compared with a mountain. What is a drop of water in an ocean? How can we compare a spark of fire with the sun? Humility prevents us from thinking that we are greater than others.

Do the things you say betray a degree of boasting? Are some of your comments self-congratulatory?

Have you done things that are unhealthy? Perhaps you have stayed awake too late at night for no good reason.

We understand that the love between husband and wife has solid lasting qualities. The same is true about God-given love for children, family, and friends. But what about your relationship with the public? Do you love your neighbor with God's love? To be honest with yourself about this, you need to imagine some of the really annoying people you have encountered. Recall the most unpleasant, pesky individuals. These are the ones who give you the greatest opportunity to practice love of neighbor, even more so if they hurt you by the things they say or do. Make a frank assessment of this. Do you love them? Do you find it difficult or impossible to love them with God's love? Do you say bad things about these people? Have you done anything against them either openly or covertly? With even a little care you will be able to reach an honest estimate of these things.

SPIRITUAL AFFECTIONS

I have asked the above questions because introspection of this kind is vital to our spiritual development. Merely probing the conscience for sins is of little help to anyone who wants to improve the devotional life. There is no need to linger inordinately on any topic. It is enough to calmly face the facts.

Get along with it. Condense the introspection into an inventory of deep desires. After pondering each question, make a general assessment of your own character.

Do you love God, others, and yourself?

Do your own sins as well as those of others disturb you?

How great is your interest in money, pleasure, and awards?

Do you trust more in the world and less in God?

Are you saddened by small losses?

Are you too pleased with worthless things?

What do you really enjoy? What passions control you? Have you missed something important?

We can diagnose our spiritual condition by examining our desires one at a time. A lute player strums across the strings to determine if any are out of tune. Then it is a matter of tightening or loosening a few strings. This is the same as considering what we love, hate, want, wish, regret, and enjoy. If we find any that are not in harmony with music in praise of God, then we can tune them with God's help.

THE RESULTS

Following this gentle introspection you will have an understanding of your present spiritual condition.

Thank God for even the slightest observable spiritual growth. Admit that you would not have improved except for God's mercy. If you fail to find any progress, admit in all humility that you alone are responsible. Praise God for helping you. Seek God's forgiveness for your failures.

Ask God to guide you and to keep you ever faithful.

Once this personal inventory is complete and you have discussed your findings with your spiritual director, continue with the directions I give below. Meditate on one a day. Use the method we now find familiar. Become aware of God's presence. Ask God to help you.

First Day

Your soul is beautiful and noble. It has the ability to comprehend both this world and the angels in heaven. It recognizes God. It can conceive eternity. It is able to relate the quality of life here with the quality of life in paradise.

Bees feed only upon flowers. Only God can satisfy the needs of the human soul. What attracts most of your interest? Really get into this question. Truthfully now, are such things worth it? Do they cause anxiety and fretful worry? We mistakenly chase the wrong things in this world. We think we will be satisfied. When we have it all, everything the world can provide, we remain unsatisfied. In the same way that Noah released a dove from his ark after the flood (Genesis 8:9), our soul finds nowhere to land and must return to its source.

Why? If your beautiful soul can know God, why do you chase after poorer things? If you can claim eternity, why be distracted with things that rust and decay? The prodigal son (Luke 15:16) despairs that he is eating with pigs when he could be at a banquet with his father. Speak to your soul: "My soul, you are made for God. Never attempt to find your satisfaction in anything other than God." Let this thought lift your spirit. Acknowledge that your soul has an eternal dimension.

Second Day

Your soul will be satisfied with nothing less than integrity and devotion. These are far more beautiful than their counterparts. Patience is superior to retaliation. Gentleness is better than anger and hostility. Haughtiness and ambition are not nearly as valuable as humility. Generosity is preferable to stinginess. Contrast love and envy, sobriety and drunkenness. Practicing a virtuous life leaves us feeling good. Vices destroy our energy and distract us.

The devout life is pleasant and enjoyable. It helps us to bear difficult times. It is eminently desirable.

Third Day

Consider the lives of saints and martyrs. They suffered much for their faith. We are made of the same flesh. Their faith was in the very God we serve. An identical potential is in us.

Fourth Day

Now think of Christ's love and how he suffered in our world. See him in Gethsemane and Calvary. His love is poured out for you. He will help you to be faithful. As he died for us, let us be prepared to die for him.

Philothea, Jesus loved you from the cross. It is he who makes the devout life a possibility for you. We can hear the same word spoken to Jeremiah, "Before I formed you in the womb I knew you, before you were born I set you apart" (Jeremiah 1:5). God mercifully prepared each one of us for a life of devotion. In the same way that an expectant mother prepares for a child not yet born, our Lord used his cross as your spiritual layette.

Dear God, this needs to be permanently fixed in our memories. Can it be that my Savior so kindly loved me? Is he aware of me as an individual as he attracts me to himself through these various incidents in my life? If so, we must value each event highly and profit from them. It is beautiful to know that God's loving awareness has considered each one of us. He loves us and provides many opportunities for our salvation. It is as though God is focusing upon one soul only. As the sun shines upon a special place on earth, it shines no less everywhere else. This is the way our Lord is aware of us and takes care of us. He loves each of us thoroughly and without distraction. This personal love is something we should never forget.

Fifth Day

Ponder God's eternal love for you. Even before our Lord Jesus Christ was crucified for your sake, God knew you would be born, loved you, and wanted you. God has loved you from the infinity of eternity. There never was a time when you were not loved. Neither will there ever be a time when God does not love you. God has brought you to this moment. He speaks through the prophet to you and to all of us, "I have loved you with an everlasting love; I have drawn you with loving-kindness" (Jeremiah 31:3).

Dear God, this present moment in my individual life has been in your thoughts forever. Impress me with understanding. Nothing in this world is more important than one individual soul, and a soul is of little value without a commitment to God.

Sixth Day

My commitment to God is like a tree that God has planted within me. He wants to irrigate it with his blood and cause it to bear fruit. It would be better to die than to permit some storm of passion to disturb its roots. I will not permit pleasure or pain to divert me from my decision to love and serve God.

Dear God, you have planted this tree in the garden of my soul. I recognize your blessing upon me. I promise to do my very best to keep the resolutions I have made. Always live in me. Never let me leave you.

Once you have considered these things, dedicate yourself to frequent prayer, participation in church, and doing good for others. This is for spiritual maintenance. Work to correct the problems you discovered in yourself. Assure yourself you will give full energy to keeping your promises to

God. Turn your desires and spirit over to God. Announce to God that you will never claim your independence again. Ask God to make you a totally new person.

Now go to your spiritual director. Openly admit the truth you have discovered about yourself. Accept the assurance of pardon he will offer. Participate in a Communion service.

Follow-Up

Begin immediately to frequently repeat the fervent words of Paul, "None of us lives to himself alone and none of us dies to himself alone. If we live, we live to the Lord; and if we die, we die to the Lord. So, whether we live or die, we belong to the Lord" (Romans 14:7-8).

Now return to your business. Do so gently. Be careful not to spill anything you have gained. Let it begin to permeate your life in a natural, effortless manner.

The world will object, Philothea, that I have told you to do so much that you will never have time for anything else. But I have not asked you to do it all every day. There will be plenty of time for the other things of life.

THREE FINAL INSTRUCTIONS

1. Repeat your resolution to live the devout life on the first day of each month.
2. Admit openly that this is your desire. Don't say that you are devout. Say you want to be devout. Feel no shame about this. If someone tells you that you can live a devout life without going through everything I have described, don't argue about it. Gently reply that you are weak and require more guidance than others.

3. Stay with it, Philothea. Time flies away. Keep your eyes on heaven. Don't throw it away for earth or the things of hell. Look at Jesus Christ and be faithful to him.

Live, Jesus! To whom, with the Father and the Holy Spirit, be all honor and glory, now and forevermore. Amen.

About the Author

B ernard Bangley is a recently retired Presbyterian minister who has written for many years. His previous books include *Growing in His Image*, *Spiritual Treasure*, *Near to the Heart of God*, and *Talks on the Song of Songs*. Educated at Hampden-Sydney College and Union Theological Seminary in Virginia, he has held pastorates from the Appalachian Mountains to Sarasota, Florida. He now lives in Lexington, Virginia, with his wife, Anna.